Jenny Bolhofner

felt & thread

3-D APPLIQUÉ & EMBROIDERY

stashBOOKS®
an imprint of C&T Publishing

PUBLISHER: Amy Barrett-Daffin

CREATIVE DIRECTOR: Gailen Runge

SENIOR EDITOR: Roxane Cerda

EDITOR: Madison Moore

TECHNICAL EDITOR: Del Walker

COVER/BOOK DESIGNER: April Mostek

PRODUCTION COORDINATOR: Tim Manibusan

ILLUSTRATOR: Kirstie Pettersen

PHOTOGRAPHY COORDINATOR: Rachel Ackley

FRONT COVER PHOTOGRAPHY by Jenny Bolhofner

PHOTOGRAPHY by Jenny Bolhofner, unless otherwise noted

Library of Congress Cataloging-in-Publication Data

Names: Bolhofner, Jenny author

Title: Felt & thread : 3-d appliqué & embroidery / Jenny Bolhofner.

Other titles: Felt and thread

Description: Lafayette, CA : Stash Books, an imprint of C&T Publishing, [2026] | Summary: "Explore this fresh combination of felt appliqué and embroidery to create a pet portrait, nostalgic house hoop, or nature-inspired design using ten projects that range in skill level"-- Provided by publisher.

Identifiers: LCCN 2026007630 | ISBN 9781644036679 trade paperback ISBN 9781644036686 ebook

Subjects: LCSH: Embroidery | Appliqué | BISAC: CRAFTS & HOBBIES / Fiber

Arts & Textiles | CRAFTS & HOBBIES / Needlework / Embroidery | LCGFT:

Patterns (Instructional works)

Classification: LCC TT771 .B654 2026 | DDC 746.44--dc23/eng/20260218

LC record available at https://lccn.loc.gov/2026007630

Printed in China

10 9 8 7 6 5 4 3 2 1

DEDICATION

For Leah, my Grams, who shared her love of crafting with me, and taught me how to tie a knot faster than anyone this side of the Mississippi.

ACKNOWLEDGMENTS

The daunting task of writing this book coincided with one of the hardest times in my life. In spite of that, the book became a reality because of the grace and strength of God, and also greatly in part to the many people behind the scenes who held me up along the way.

Thank you to my husband, Derrick, who has always believed in me and has supported my business for over a decade. To my daughters, Olive and Hazel, thank you for being patient through the long days and nights of writing, stitching, and photographing. Your sweet hugs got me through.

Thank you to my family who fostered my love of art from a young age. To my Mom, Cindy, and my Grams, Leah, thank you for always inspiring me, checking in (especially on the hard days), and believing in me throughout this entire project. To my Dad, David, thank you for bringing me along to pottery classes all those years ago, and for paving the way through the publishing world. To my husband's whole family, thank you for being my cheerleaders during the ups and downs of the writing process.

To Monica, Jen, Kelsey, Em, Jill, Noel, Sarah and my many mom friends (you know who you are), thank you for letting me vent without judgement and lifting me up on the hard days. To my online community of fiber artists and craft enthusiasts, thank you for always inspiring me and cheering me on. Without your constant encouragement to keep creating, I wouldn't be where I am today.

To Nicole, who taught me the value of drawing every day, thank you. You were always more than a professor to me. You were a mentor and role model.

Thank you to my incredible editor, Madison, who sought me out when I thought writing a book was just a pipedream. I am forever grateful for your patience and encouragement. Thank you to the entire C&T Publishing team for guiding me through the publication process.

A special thank you to Crystal and Renae of Benzie Design for supplying me with the most luxurious felt and embroidery tools, and to Kate at Modern Hoopla for your beautifully handmade frames and hoop props.

And I would be remiss if I did not thank my trusty needles for getting me through all of the hours of stitching needed to write this book. Many metallic warhorses were bent and broken, but will never be forgotten.

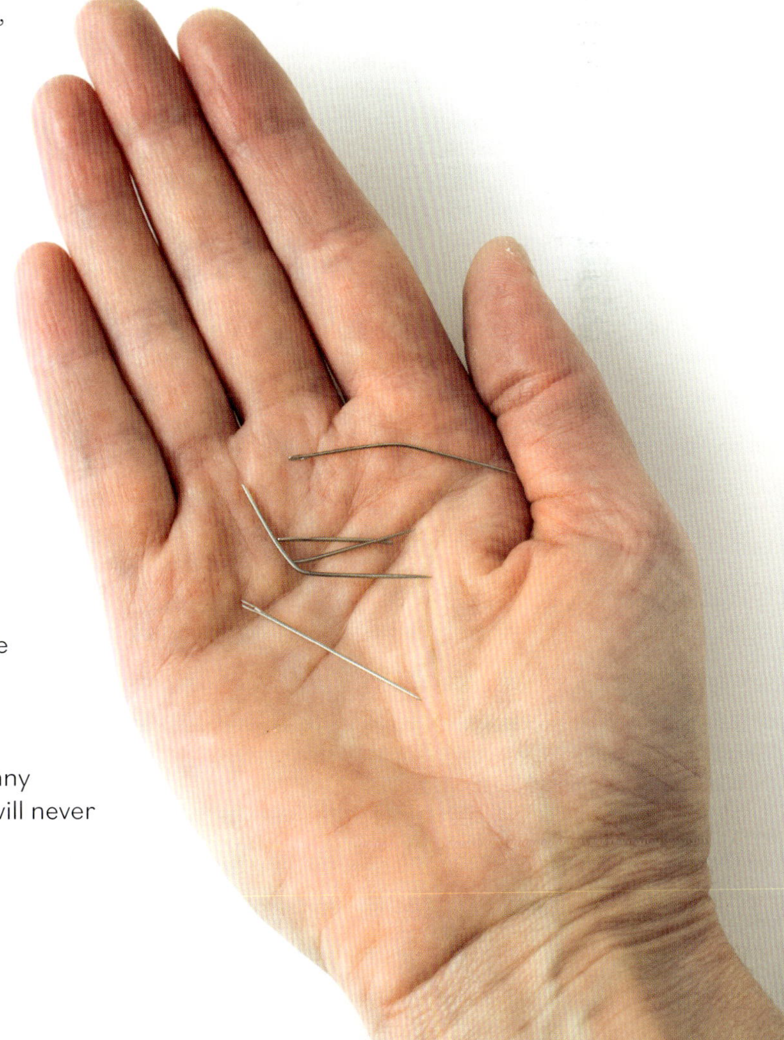

contents

PROJECTS

HOUSE PORTRAITS

PET PORTRAITS

MUSHROOMS

INSECTS

OCEAN CREATURES

introduction

Fiber art has come a long way from the days of Victorian samplers. Today, textiles and thread are being manipulated and challenged beyond their typical two dimensionality. On their own, felt and thread can be seen as basic, maybe even uninteresting materials. Yet together, through appliqué and embroidery, they can create captivating pieces of fiber engineering. I hope that this book builds your confidence in trying innovative processes and challenges any preconceptions about felt art.

The projects in this book explore how texture, color, and depth can be used to bring a subject to life. You'll study the fundamentals, like composition, color theory, and layering. You'll learn how to combine those basics with techniques like felt appliqué and embroidery, to create dynamic, sculptural pieces. Just as stitching each project is about building up layers, the skills you learn in this book will continue to compound. I know you will be emboldened to create your own projects after tackling these new skills. I hope you enjoy stitching along with me and (quite literally) elevating your felt and embroidery game. I trust that this book will allow you to slow down, observe, and take time for intentional crafting. May you never have to rethread your needle, and your only knots be intentional ones!

FELT APPLIQUÉ

Felt appliqué is the technique of attaching a piece of felt to another piece of fabric or felt. Appliquéing layers of felt is fundamental to achieving a three-dimensional effect.

EMBROIDERY

While felt appliqué is essential for building physical depth, embroidering on top of layers is the key to building visual depth. Incorporating a variety of stitches builds texture and makes an object appear more realistic. Nature itself is never all the same texture! Varying thread thickness and stitch direction also helps make things more dimensional. Finally, thread painting allows you to achieve realistic, blended stitches that mimic the art of painting.

***NOTE:** The combination of felt appliqué and overlaid embroidery is often referred to as padded stumpwork. Felt layers provide a padded foundation for embroidery, creating a three dimensional effect.*

Embroidery Needles
HIROSHIMA NEEDLE
Milly

tools & materials

When it comes to tools and materials, the old adage, "You get what you pay for," definitely applies. There are certainly economical, readily available supplies out there (I'm looking at you, acrylic craft felt), and these may be a great place to start if you are just wanting to practice. But, most cheap supplies will not be durable and might cause more frustration in the long run.

Investing in higher quality tools and materials makes a huge difference. Having the right supplies can make your crafting experience more enjoyable and more efficient. Better quality tools also stand the test of time, which is important when you are creating artistic keepsakes. If you are spending the time and energy to create a masterpiece, you don't want to see that all go to waste just because the materials you used aren't long-lasting.

For the majority of my felt and embroidery needs, I use supplies from Benzie Design. In addition to high quality felt, they offer a wide variety of tools, from scissors and needles, to floss and stuffing tools.

FELT

While acrylic craft felt is inexpensive and widely available at your local craft chains, I recommend using only wool and wool blend felt. Acrylic felt does not hold up well when transferring templates because the fibers stretch too easily, and iron-reliant transfer methods are nearly impossible because the heat can melt the synthetic fibers. It also tends to pill and look ratty over time. If you choose to use acrylic felt, please only iron with a low heat setting and non-stick plate.

Wool and wool blend felt is more durable and heat resistant, which is vital for many template transfer techniques. I use only wool and wool blend felt from Benzie Design because it is strong enough to withstand manipulation like heating, bending, creasing, and repeated layering. Wool and wool blend felt also cuts more smoothly for more intricate pieces, which ensures less fraying and more accurate detail.

Comparing wool felt to acrylic felt is like comparing a box of 64 Crayola crayons to the four pack of crayons you get with the kids menu at a restaurant. There is generally a larger variety of colors for wool felt than acrylic felt. You can find anything from subtle, natural dyes, to more robust, bold color choices.

THREAD CONDITIONER
BENZIE DESIGN

THREAD

I highly recommend using DMC six stranded cotton embroidery thread. It is a high quality thread. It doesn't break easily when pulled, and it glides through felt smoothly. DMC thread also comes in such a wide range of colors; you are sure to find something that will match any felt you are using.

Most importantly, I like the option of being able to divide the six strands to vary the thickness of stitches. This is very important when creating depth in embroidery. Just like drawing, where you rely on varying line thicknesses to help convey emphasis in certain areas, you need to be able to stitch with different thread thicknesses. A single stranded french knot is perfect for the smallest eye sparkle in a pet portrait, while a full six strands are required to create bold landscaping in a house portrait.

THREAD CONDITIONER

When overlaying embroidery on multiple felt appliqué layers, beeswax thread conditioner is good to have on hand to keep your thread from knotting or fraying. It is also helpful when stitching through wash-away stabilizer transfer paper to keep the thread from getting any residue on it.

NEEDLES

While I occasionally use DMC embroidery needles because they are readily available and come in a wide size range, I prefer to use Tulip embroidery needles most of the time. Tulip needles have a little more spring in the body, which allows them to bend more without breaking (something that is very important when you are testing the limits of thick layers as you embroider). They also have gold plated eyes that are easier to thread and that glide much more smoothly through layers of felt.

Tulip embroidery needles come in varying sizes, from 3 to 10. DMC embroidery needles range from 1 to 10. The smaller the number, the thicker the needle and the larger the eye hole. If you use all six strands of embroidery floss or are passing through a substantial number of layers, choose a smaller numbered (thicker) needle. If you use just a single strand of thread or are passing through just one or two layers of felt, use a larger numbered (thinner) embroidery needle.

SCISSORS

Scissors are one of the most important tools in my arsenal. They can be the difference between producing crisp shapes and churning out indistinguishable felt blobs. Felt scissors are my jack-of-all-trade scissors because they can cut through felt and embroidery thread with equal smoothness. Fiskars Micro-Tip scissors do an excellent job of cutting the most precise and intricate edges. Their stainless steel beveled edged blades slice through felt like butter. But, if you are only purchasing one pair, I suggest Kai N5000 scissors. They are efficient in cutting large pieces of felt, but handle the tiny, more complicated shapes just as well. They have ergonomic handles that make repetitive cutting much more comfortable. Plus the blades stay sharp for years!

You may also want to consider embroidery scissors or thread snips, as they fit into smaller spaces and snip the tiniest of excess threads. Be warned: they are not sturdy enough to slice through felt.

TRANSFER TOOLS

See Transferring Templates (page 19) for more on using each kind of tool.

Frixion Heat Erasable Pen

Frixion pens from Pilot are a wonderful way to transfer most patterns because they require the least amount of prep work and provide instant gratification. However, they are not a suitable method when using dark colored felt as the ink is not visible.

Water Soluble Pencil

If you enjoy the ease of a Frixion pen, but need to transfer templates to a dark colored felt, a white water soluble pencil is a useful tool. However, because these pencils have a wider tip and require more pressure when tracing, it is not adequate for transferring intricate patterns.

NOTE: *Water soluble pencils are handy to have for more than just transferring templates. They can be used to add smooth, subtle highlights to portraits.*

Freezer Paper

I love using freezer paper for several reasons: it requires no pre-soaking, it works on every color of felt, and you can reuse the templates dozens of times. It is also the most precise way to transfer templates, which is important when working with smaller pieces. Quilter's Freezer Paper by C&T Publishing comes in printable sheets, or you can buy freezer paper by the roll from most grocery store chains. The rolled freezer paper is handy for projects that have templates larger than printer paper size.

Wash-Away Stabilizer Transfer Paper

I prefer to use wash-away stabilizer paper for intricate embroidery on top of felt layers. Think of it as a paint by numbers for embroidery, providing guidelines to stitch along. While this method does require some prep work, it is fairly simple and perfect for detailed stitching and text. There are many brands of water soluble paper available, but I personally like to use Sticky Fabri-Solvy.

Tracing Vellum

If you're working from a physical photo or digital device, images are sometimes too dark to trace directly onto freezer paper. Tracing vellum is clearer and thick enough that it can also be used as a template to trace with a Frixion pen. Vellum can be a useful interim transfer tool as well. You can trace images onto it, and then trace the vellum images onto freezer paper or wash-away paper.

NOTE: *If you are new to felt appliqué and acquiring necessary tools, I would suggest starting out by purchasing freezer paper and a Frixion pen. Both are simple to use, readily available, inexpensive, and cover the majority of the template transfers in this book.*

Iron

Having an iron is good for smoothing wrinkled felt and is an imperative tool for Frixion pen and freezer paper transfers. For larger projects, I prefer the Hamilton Beach non-stick iron. It has multiple heat settings, an extra-glide nonstick soleplate and a retractable cord for easy storage.

For smaller, more intricate pieces, I suggest using the Oliso M3Pro Project Iron. It has a non-stick heat plate for smooth use, a built-in LED light to help focus on your work, and a 2″ detailer tip that works great for tight corners and creasing tiny felt pieces. The temperature controls also allow you to use it on both acrylic and wool felt.

TRACING SOURCES

Lightbox

I use a lightbox to transfer hand-drawn images and handwriting onto freezer paper, wash-away stabilizer transfer paper, or tracing paper/vellum. It requires little to no setup and is a consistent light source for even tracing. Using a window is a free and widely available alternative if you do not have a lightbox, though it is daytime dependent and can be trickier.

Digital Device

In some instances, you may be working from an image on a digital device. If you want to copy it directly, I suggest turning your brightness up to max level and keeping all other lighting in the environment off. Use tracing vellum and a pencil or felt tip marker to trace the image.

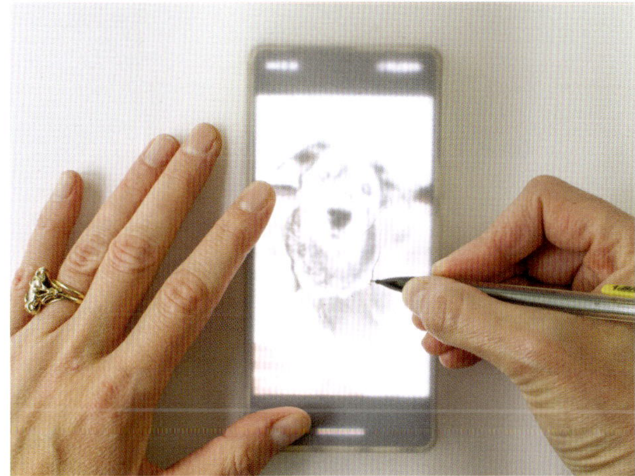

ART MARKERS

I use art markers sparingly, but they come in handy for certain projects. I like to use Tombow ABT Pro double sided markers. They are great for staining wooden hoops to match a project's color palette. Occasionally, I use them for light shading in portraits, specifically around the tongue, mouth, and ears of an animal. Because those areas of a portrait tend to be smoother than the rest, stitching details in those areas adds too much texture and looks unnatural. Adding just a hint of shading with an art marker looks more polished and realistic.

ADHESIVES

Hot Glue

Hot glue is the simplest, and fastest way to bond felt. I prefer this method unless I am trying to bond something with a little more weight, or if I need to adhere felt to a different material such as plastic or metal.

E6000

E6000 adhesive bonds to more materials and is a stronger alternative to hot glue. Waterproof, temperature-resistant, and flexible, it is perfect if you need to bond wood, plastic, or metal to felt. This glue can be harder to control with small pieces and the drying time is longer than hot glue, so it is important to hold items in place or lay them flat for 24 hours to cure properly.

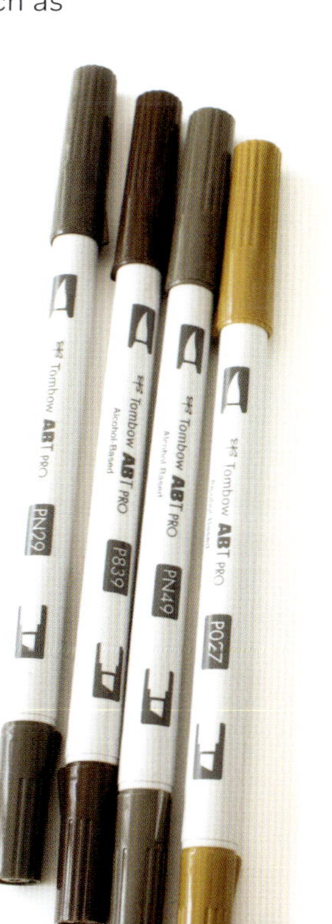

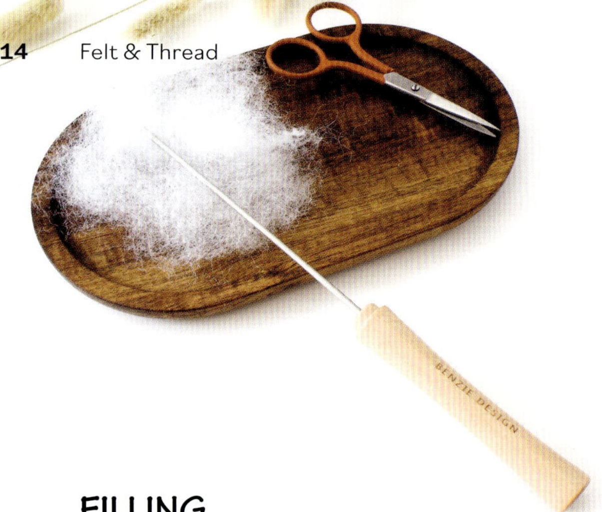

FILLING

For the majority of my projects, I use polyester filling because it is consistent, not lumpy, and easy to pack into small spaces. There are many different kinds to choose from, but I mainly use Poly-Fil because of the quality and availability. If you prefer, you can cut your felt scraps and/or threads down into tiny bits and use them as stuffing.

STUFFING TOOL

I use the Benzie Design stuffing tool when padding my designs. It has a narrow, stainless steel crown tip that grabs a hold of filling to transfer it effortlessly into tight spaces.

HOOPS

I use beechwood hoops with brass clasps as they are much more durable than bamboo hoops, which tend to splinter and warp. Plastic hoops are another option, but I personally like the aesthetic of a more natural material—especially when it comes to subject matter that is more aligned with nature.

FRAMES AND PROPS

As beautiful as a piece may be, it can sometimes look unfinished in its original hoop. For a more polished look, I use frames and props from Modern Hoopla. Frames come in multiple sizes, shapes and stains. Hoop Props are a simple display option and a nice alternative to traditional wall hanging. These also come in various stains, but are only recommended for hoops up to 6″ in diameter.

MISCELLANEOUS TOOLS

Lint Roller

One of the most underrated tools in my arsenal is a lint roller. It is the last thing I use on a project to ensure there are no stray hairs or fuzz.

Stiffy Fabric Stiffener

Sometimes, in order to obtain sculptural goals with thread and felt, you need a little help. Plaid brand Stiffy Fabric Stiffener is a wonderful tool to make fibers sturdy, yet still pliable. Paint a thin layer and remove any excess glue. Allow painted felt or thread to dry for 30–45 minutes.

Pliers

Precision flat nose pliers are good to have on hand when you are stitching through multiple layers of felt (usually 7 or more layers). You can use them to gently grab the needle and pull it through. Pliers are also handy for tightening hoop clasps and for bending small pieces of felt to create ruffled edges.

TEMPLATES

All of the projects require templates. To access them, scan the included QR code or go to **tinyurl.com/11646-patterns-download** Each project notes which templates are needed, and the templates are clearly labeled with the names used in the project instructions.

Assortment of Modern Hoopla hoops and frames

basic felt techniques

Before diving straight into the projects in this book, it's important to go over some felt fundamentals. These skills will lay the groundwork for any project you want to tackle.

CHOOSING FELT COLORS

The color choices of a project are arguably just as important as the subject itself. Color evokes feeling and can elicit certain psychological responses, so it's important to select them carefully.

Mood

In portraiture and still lifes, you often try to use colors that are true to the objects you are depicting. However, you can play with the mood of the portrait by simply varying the shades of colors. If you wish to inspire feelings of nostalgia, muted colors help represent that vibe. If you are stitching something you want to come off as playful or bold, it's important to choose more vibrant colors. Even if you choose to represent your subject matter in its true colors, play around with background colors to help give the overall piece a certain mood.

The bright blues of the mussel are reminiscent of a sunny day at the beach, while the muted background of the moth evokes the subtle light of evening.

Quilter's
freezer paper
sheets
8½" × 11"
FISKARS
CITRON
DMC581
EVERGREEN
DMC890

Using a Color Wheel

Choosing a color palette is my first step in any project. First, choose the most predominant color of the piece. Once you have a main color, select accent colors that help the subject matter stand out, but that are also cohesive with the overall feel of the project.

Choosing a specific color scheme strategy with the color wheel can help:

Monochromatic: Use tints, shades and tones of a single color.

Complementary: Use colors opposite each other on the color wheel.

Analogous: Use up to three neighboring colors on the color wheel.

Split-Complementary: Use a main color, its complementary color, and the complementary color's neighbor.

Triadic: Use three colors equidistant from one another on the color wheel.

Let's use the Sputnik Sea Urchin project as an example. First, I chose the purple shell as the main color. The seaweed details brought in shades of green, which set me up with a complementary palette. I decided to go further and use a split-complementary color strategy, adding in a muted yellow (green's neighbor) for the background.

C&T Publishing Essential Color Wheel Companion by Joen Wolfrem and Sputnik Sea Urchin (page 154)

Split-complementary color palette for the Sputnik Sea Urchin

Color Swatches

Once you have a basic understanding of which colors you plan to use, I find it handy to use Benzie Design swatch charts to finalize felt colors. There are 90 color swatches for their wool blend felt and 72 for their Bellwether pure wool felt. They are given a corresponding DMC floss color to make color matching effortless. The swatches are spread across multiple pages which helps to overlay them and get a feel for what colors work best together.

CREATING A BACKGROUND

Deciding whether the background of your project should be detailed or minimalistic is really up to personal preference. In some instances, adding details helps enhance the subject matter or helps to add to the story telling of a piece. Including a miniature version of your dog's favorite toy in the background of his portrait might be the best way to bring in his personality. Or, you might want to make sure a tree that is no longer standing is memorialized in the background of a house portrait. But choosing just one focal point, with no extraneous details, can also be powerful; a contrasting background color choice can complete a piece that might otherwise seem plain.

Composition of Subject

The placement of the subject matter within your hoop is just as important as choosing the right colors. The obvious choice for most projects is to place the subject in the center, as it is symmetrically pleasing. Sometimes having more negative space above, below, or to the side of a subject makes it more engaging, especially with a simple background, but always keep balance and focus in mind. For example, if you place the subject to one side and surround it with lots of detail, the focal point may be hard to pick out, so if you are creating an intricate background, consider centering the main subject.

TRANSFERRING TEMPLATES

There are many different ways to transfer templates to felt. I suggest trying the methods that appeal to you to see what you prefer. See Transfer Tools (page 11) for more on these materials.

Frixion Heat Erasable Pen Transfer

When it's time to erase these heat-soluble marks, be aware that a hair dryer is a safer method if you're using acrylic felt. For wool felt, make sure your iron is set accordingly. This transfer method does not work on darker colored felt. It is also less effective for really intricate pieces.

***TIP:** The Frixion pen is a great tool if you need to transfer multiples of the same template. It is much faster to trace the same template many times than to use the freezer paper method.*

1 Place the template onto the felt, and trace around it with the pen.

2 Cut around the drawn lines.

3 Erase the marks with an iron or hair dryer.

***NOTE:** Please be aware that Frixion pen marks may reappear if they are exposed to extremely cold temperatures (such as being mailed during winter months). You can erase marks again with an iron or hair dryer.*

Water Soluble Pencil Transfer

Some felt dyes can bleed, and wool fibers can shrink with water. To avoid shrinking and color bleeding, pre-soak the felt and allow it to air dry before using this method.

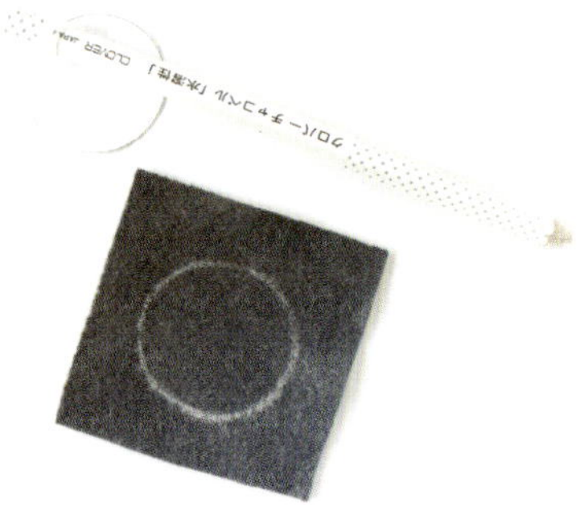

1 Place the template onto the felt, and trace around it with the pencil.

2 Cut around the drawn lines, then rinse away the lines.

Freezer Paper Transfer

Print your templates directly onto Quilter's Freezer Paper Sheets, or lay a sheet of freezer paper over the pattern and trace it with a pencil. Be sure to print or draw on the matte side of the paper. The shiny side adheres to the felt. You can reuse freezer paper templates dozens of times, so I recommend labeling them.

1 Trace, draw, or print the design onto the freezer paper.

2 Lay the paper onto the felt shiny side down. Iron to the felt, using the correct heat setting for the kind of felt.

3 Cut the shape out around the paper, then peel the paper off the felt. Be sure to pull the paper off gently so you don't distort the shape.

***NOTE:** Acrylic felt is not the best felt to use for this method. The iron would need to be set to a low setting to avoid melting the fibers, and lower heat settings do not work well for bonding freezer paper. Plus, peeling the paper from acrylic felt often misshapes the lower-quality fibers.*

Wash-Away Stabilizer Transfer Paper

Wash-away paper (like Sticky Fabri-Solvy) is a great tool for transferring intricate embroidery designs. It is extremely important to pre-soak the entire sheet of felt with this method. Doing so will help prevent color bleeding and shrinking. Soaking before cutting also ensures all pieces shrink at the same rate.

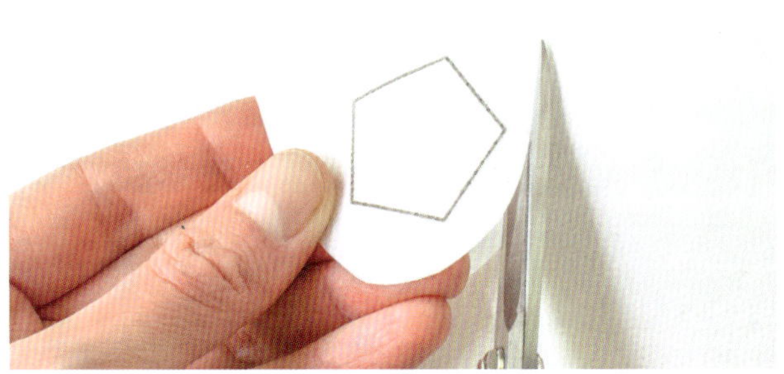

1 Trace, draw, or print the design onto the wash-away paper. Cut out the shapes with extra space around them.

2 Peel the paper away, and adhere the sticky sheet to the felt.

3 Stitch over the design as instructed by the project.

4 Soak and rinse off the wash-away paper.

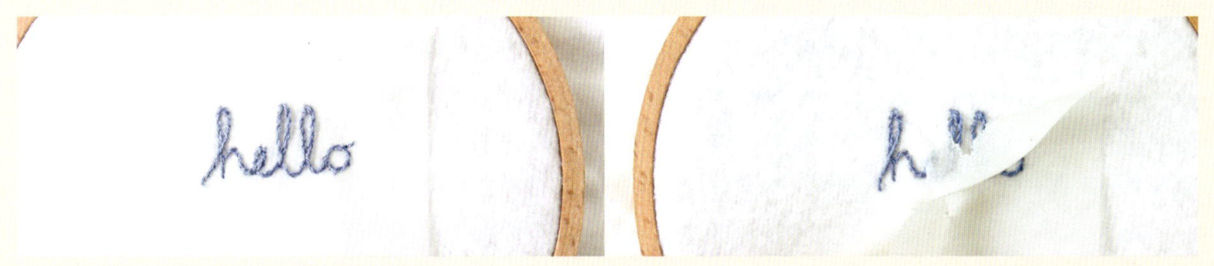

***TIP:** If you're in a pinch, tracing paper can work in a similar way to wash-away paper for simple stitched lines, like text. Trace the letters onto the paper. Lay the paper over the felt, then stitch on top. Gently tear the paper away.*

LAYERING FELT

Having a background in printmaking, I often approach my felt projects like I would a print, working from background to foreground, layering colors and shapes. I ask myself, what part of my image is the farthest away? What parts are sticking out the closest to me? What parts do I want to show the most of, and which do I want to be slightly covered?

Working from background to foreground (and often largest piece of felt to smallest piece of felt), creates depth, dimension, and perspective. In the Edwin Dog Portrait (page 70), the body of the animal is portrayed as being farther away than the face, which is looking up out of the hoop. The largest piece of felt is cut for the hind quarters, then slightly smaller pieces for the front of the body, and then even smaller pieces for the dog's face.

CUTTING PIECES

Accuracy is key when cutting felt pieces. Making sure that edges line up where they are supposed to and covering previous layers precisely, is key to creating a three dimensional effect. Using tools like freezer paper and Fiskars Micro-Tip scissors help achieve this level of accuracy (see Tools and Materials, page 8).

FELT APPLIQUÉ

Once felt pieces are traced and cut, they need to be stabilized in a technique called felt appliqué. While some artists glue their felt layers down as they work, I prefer to stitch them. I find that glue makes it too hard to push a needle through when it comes time to add embroidery. Stitching is also more secure and flattens the pieces down, making them appear more cohesive.

There are several different stitches that you can use for felt appliqué. The running stitch is the most basic, and good for adding multiple layers. The blanket stitch is the sturdiest and best at closing the seams of felt edging. A whip stitch is another good option that closes the outside edges and lends a different aesthetic.

***NOTE:** Many of the projects in this book are made up of dozens of pieces. In order to ensure you know which piece is which after cutting them out, I suggest labeling them with the correct template letter and number. You can do this by using a heat erasable pen or water soluble pencil to mark the felt directly. Pinning each felt piece with a post-it note is another option. Or if the pieces are very small, you can lay them out onto a sheet of paper or their respective template page and label them underneath.*

***TIP:** When cutting small or intricate pieces, turn the felt while holding the scissors in place. Aside from opening and closing the blades, the scissors should remain in the same spot while you rotate the felt.*

basic embroidery techniques

While felt layering is the foundation of the portrait projects, embroidery is the key to bringing them to life. Embroidery provides texture, detail, and color variation.

COLOR CHOICES FOR THREAD

The driving force behind choosing thread colors is the color of the felt foundations. For most felt appliqué, you want to match the thread color as closely as possible to the felt being stitched. The other thread colors used in a project come down to how closely you want to replicate your subject matter, the mood of the project, and whether you want to blend or add contrast.

Color Charts

There are two tools that I highly recommend when choosing thread colors. The first is the Benzie Design Swatch Charts that have a DMC floss color printed below each felt color, taking the guesswork out of color matching. I would also recommend using a DMC Printed Color Card. It has rectangular swatches of all of the six stranded floss colors, along with some specialty floss colors, which are grouped in color families rather than in numerical order. This is helpful because you can find tints and shades of colors you are already using, as well as explore other colors that might complement those colors.

Blending vs. Contrasting

All projects, no matter the subject, need areas of both thread blending and contrast. Blended areas give your eyes a place to settle, while contrast draws your attention. It's crucial to recognize which parts of your project should play which role. For example, when stitching fur in pet portraits, the color transitions should be smooth to replicate the texture of the animal. But for eye areas, choose stark, contrasting thread colors like black and white to make them pop as the focal point of the portrait.

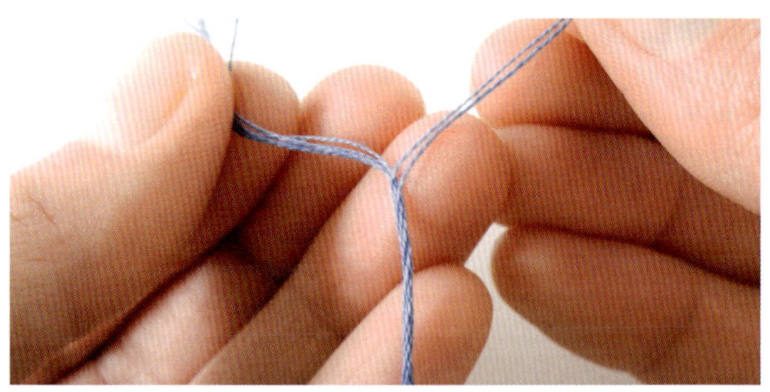

SPLITTING THREAD

DMC cotton embroidery thread is composed of six strands which can be divided to vary stitch thickness. Splitting the thread into a different number of strands is one of the simplest, yet effective ways to create different textures and depths in your projects.

Separate the number of strands you want at the top. Gently pull the strands apart down the length of the piece of thread.

STITCH LIBRARY

Revisit these step-by-step stitch instructions as needed while working on the projects.

Straight Stitch

The straight stitch is the most basic embroidery stitch, which also makes it very versatile. It can be made horizontally, vertically, or at an angle.

1 Bring the needle up through the felt. Then, bring the needle back down through the felt about 3⁄16″ (the length of the stitch) from the first hole.

Running Stitch

Running stitch is the main stitch used in these projects to appliqué the felt pieces onto each other and the hoop.

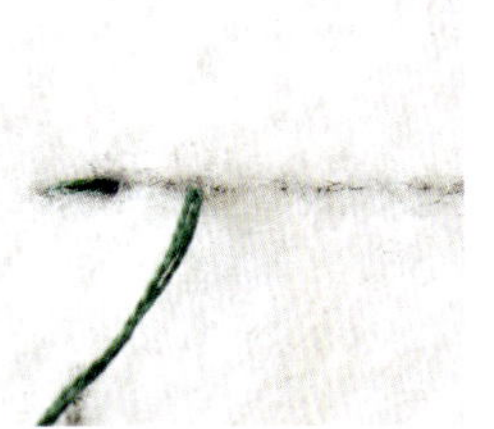

1 Create a single straight stitch. Bring the needle up through the felt about 1⁄4″ away from the first stitch. Bring the needle back down to create another straight stitch.

2 Continue creating a line of straight stitches with a 1⁄4″ gap between each one.

Seed Stitch

Seed stitch is great for creating texture. The small stitches can be randomly placed at various angles, or slanted in the same direction to create a unified texture, like for fur in a pet portrait.

1 Make a small, diagonal straight stitch.

2 Continue to make small straight stitches at various angles, filling the desired area.

Cross Stitch

Cross stitches can be used to add pattern and texture. When making this stitch, imagine working within small boxes.

1 Bring the needle up through the felt and make a diagonal straight stitch starting at the lower left corner of the "box" and ending in the upper right corner of the "box".

2 Create a second diagonal straight stitch over the first one, starting in the lower right corner of the "box" and ending in the upper left corner to create an *X*. Repeat as desired to create a row or fill a space.

Back Stitch

Backstitches create a crisp, solid line, and can be used to join two pieces of fabric more permanently than with a running stitch.

1 Make a straight stitch.

2 Bring the needle up one stitch length away from the first stitch. Bring it down through the second hole of the previous stitch. Repeat to create a line of stitches.

Stem Stitch

Stem stitch creates a beautiful rope-like texture and is perfect for flowing text and organic outlines.

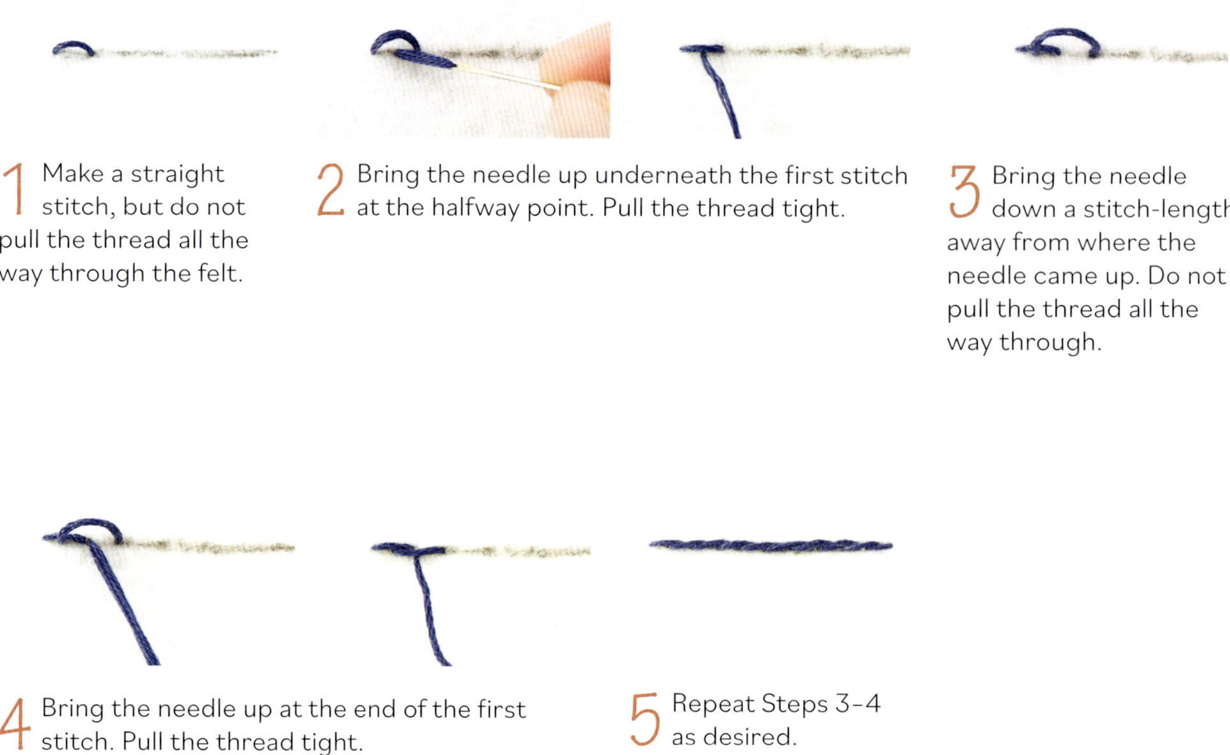

1 Make a straight stitch, but do not pull the thread all the way through the felt.

2 Bring the needle up underneath the first stitch at the halfway point. Pull the thread tight.

3 Bring the needle down a stitch-length away from where the needle came up. Do not pull the thread all the way through.

4 Bring the needle up at the end of the first stitch. Pull the thread tight.

5 Repeat Steps 3–4 as desired.

Split Backstitch

Split backstitch adds rich texture and thickness to a basic backstitch. It is also a wonderful stitch for following curved lines. I suggest using an even number of threads (2, 4 or 6) for this stitch so that when you split it with the needle, it is divided evenly.

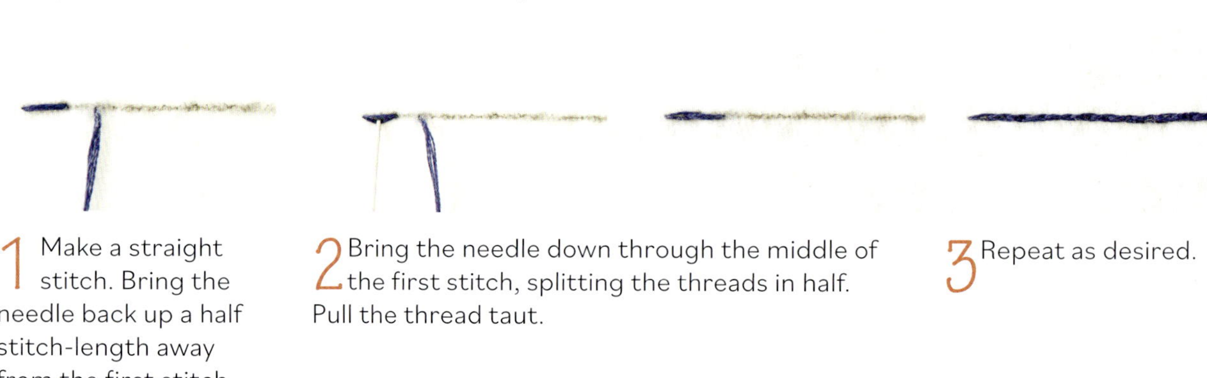

1 Make a straight stitch. Bring the needle back up a half stitch-length away from the first stitch.

2 Bring the needle down through the middle of the first stitch, splitting the threads in half. Pull the thread taut.

3 Repeat as desired.

Whip Stitch

Whip stitch is good for attaching two pieces and closing seams. It also has a little more give than a blanket stitch (below), which comes in handy for some projects.

1 Layer two pieces of felt on top of each other. From in between the two pieces, bring the needle out through one piece, about 3⁄16″ below the edge, sandwiching the knot.

2 Bring the needle up to the top of both pieces so it wraps around the outside edges. Then, stitch down through both pieces at a slight diagonal angle, about 3⁄16″ over from the first stitch.

3 Repeat Step 2 around the entire edge.

Blanket Stitch

Blanket stitch is used to attach two or more pieces of felt or decorate an edge. Its scalloped border completely seals felt edges, making it more ornate and durable than the simple whip stitch.

1 Layer two pieces of felt on top of each other. From in between the two pieces, bring the needle out through one piece, about 3⁄16″ below the edge, sandwiching the knot.

2 Bring the needle up to the top of both pieces so it wraps around the outside edges. Stitch the needle down through the top in the same hole as Step 1. Don't pull the thread tight.

3 Pass the needle through the loop made in Step 2, and pull the thread tight.

4 Bring the needle down through the piece of felt, about ¼″ from the previous stitch. Do not pull the loop tight yet.

5 Pass the needle back through the loop from behind. Pull tight. Repeat Steps 4–5 around the entire edge.

Blanket Stitch Appliqué

A blanket stitch can also be used to attach a smaller piece of felt on top of a larger one in this appliqué technique.

1 Bring the needle up through both pieces of felt about ⅛″ from the edge of the top piece.

2 Bring the needle down directly across from where you came up, wrapping over the edge of the top piece of felt. Don't pull the thread tight. Bring the needle back up beside the hole you just went down, and pass the needle through the loop. Pull the thread tight.

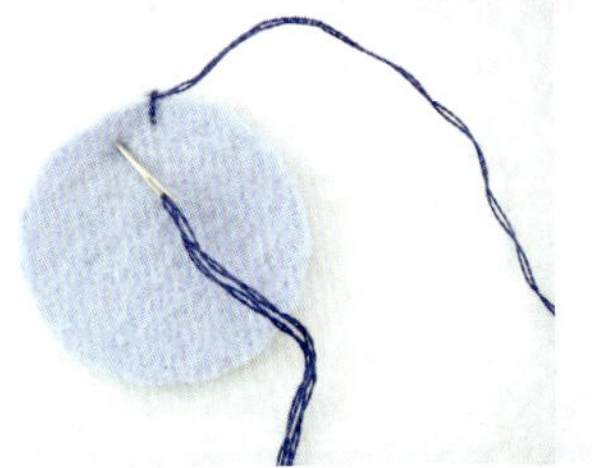

3 Bring the needle down through both layers of felt, about 3⁄16″ to the left of the first stitch. Don't pull the thread tight, but leave a small loop.

4 Bring the needle up through the base felt, along the edge of the top felt, directly across from where you came down with the needle in Step 3.

5 Pass the needle through the loop, and then pull tight.

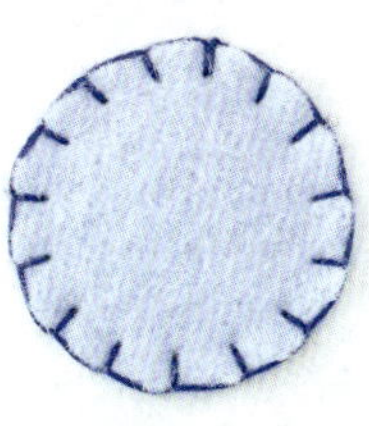

6 Repeat Steps 3–5 to around the edge of the top felt. When you return to the starting point, bring your needle down through the top edge of the first stitch to secure it.

Satin Stitch

Satin stitch is a great way to fill smooth, solid areas.

***TIP:** When using satin stitch, it's sometimes easier to start in the middle of a large section and work outward in one direction and then outward in the other. This helps keep the stitches more even and flat.*

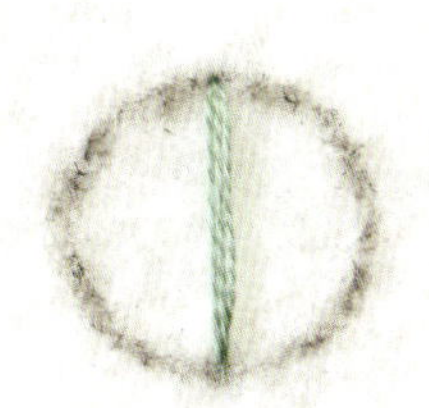
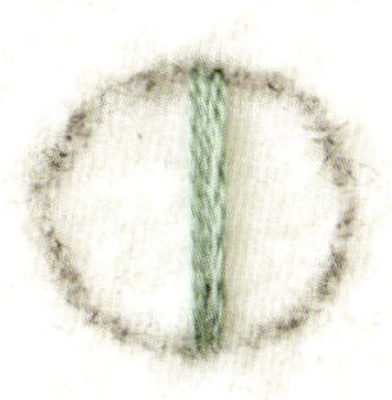

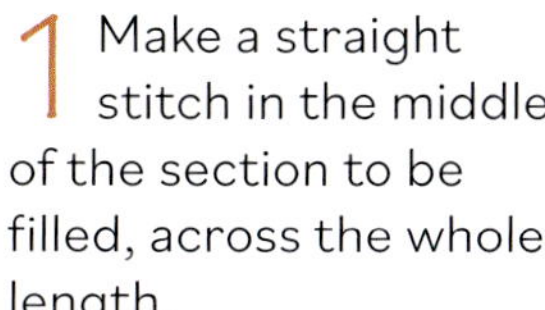

1 Make a straight stitch in the middle of the section to be filled, across the whole length.

2 Bring the needle up next to the stitch you just made, being sure to come up on the same side you did for the first stitch. Create another straight stitch next to the first stitch.

3 Repeat Step 2 until you have filled half of the section.

4 Fill the other side of the section by repeating Step 2, again starting in the middle.

French Knot

French knots add a great contrasting texture or the perfect pop of decoration to a piece. Vary the size of a French knot by using more strands or wrapping the needle and thread more than twice—the more wraps, the larger the knot.

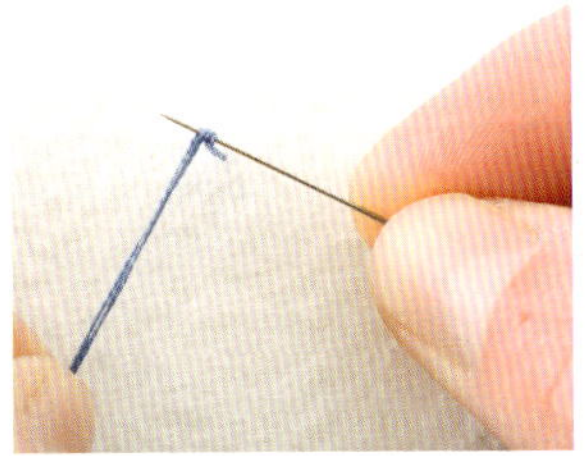

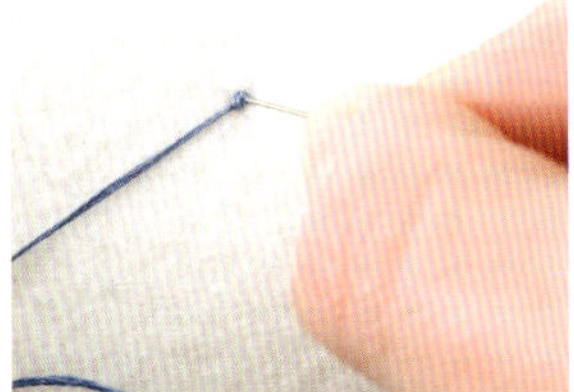

1 Bring the needle up through the felt with your dominant hand. With your non-dominant hand, hold the thread taut and off to the side. Wrap the needle around the thread twice with your dominant hand.

2 Still holding the thread taut in your non-dominant hand, bring the needle down through the felt close to, but not directly in, the hole you came up through.

3 Pull the needle through, keeping the thread taut until you can no longer hold it at the base of the knot. Let go, and pull the knot tight to cinch.

TIP: *French knots can be tricky at first because they require both hands to work at the same time, each doing something very different. The key is to keep the thread that is in your non-dominant hand taut until the very end when it is time to pull the thread tight. If you let go too soon, you will end up with a sloppy, loose knot.*

Feather Stitch

Feather stitch is good for adding flourishes or for landscape texturing. To practice this stitch, use a Frixion pen to draw three parallel lines, spaced about 3⁄16″ apart.

1 Bring the needle up at the base of the line on the left, then bring it down at the base of the second line. Don't pull the thread tight.

2 Bring the needle up on the middle line, about 3⁄16″ from where the needle went down in the previous stitch.

3 Pass the needle through the loop of thread in Step 1. Pull tight.

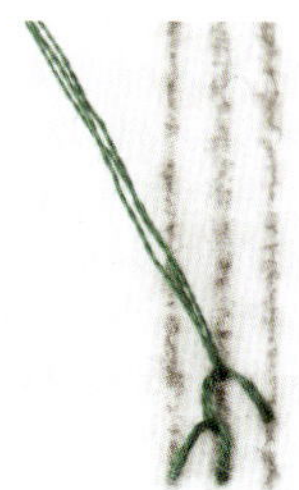

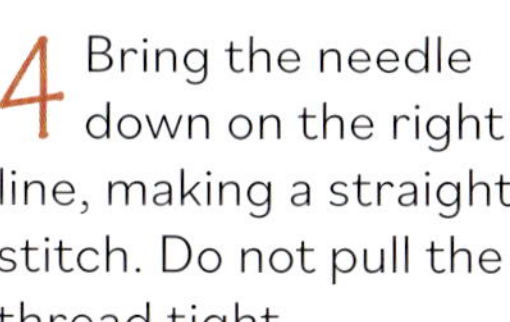

4 Bring the needle down on the right line, making a straight stitch. Do not pull the thread tight.

5 Bring the needle up on the middle line about 3⁄16″ from where the needle went down in the previous stitch. Pass the needle through the loop in Step 4. Pull tight.

6 Repeat Steps 4–5, alternating the straight stitch loops from left to right.

Long and Short Stitch

Long and short stitch is the best way to subtly blend thread colors for thread painting. I suggest using 1–2 strands of floss because it is much easier to naturally integrate colors with thinner strands. Varying stitch length will also give your stitching a more natural look and make for smoother color transitions.

You may choose to work from darker thread color to lighter, or vice versa—it is up to you. For this example, I blended three shades, starting with the darkest color and working to the lightest one.

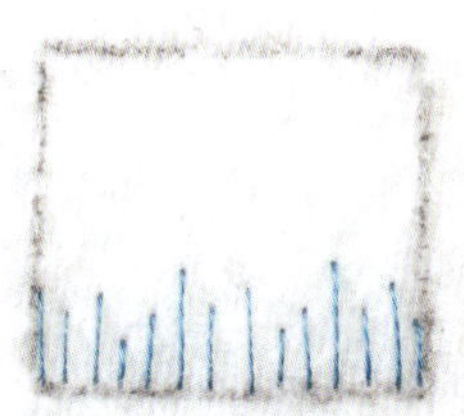

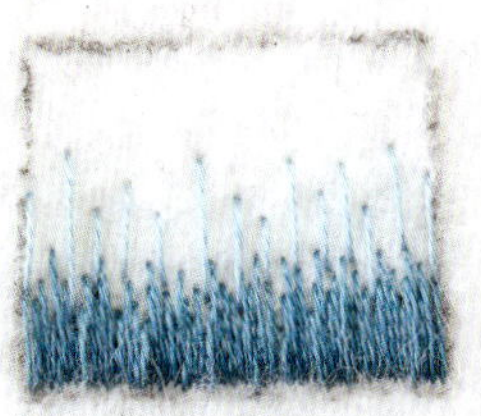

1 Add straight stitches of varying lengths across the base of the stitch area with the darkest color.

2 Go back in and fill in the gaps between the stitches with the same color, again being sure to vary the length of the straight stitches.

3 Using the next lightest thread color, make vertical straight stitches that attach to the stitches from Steps 1–2 (add a short stitch connecting to an existing long stitch and vice versa. Make sure to continue varying the stitch length.

4 Repeat Step 3 with the lightest thread color to fill in the rest of the area.

Brick Stitch

Brick stitch creates a beautifully textured, staggered stitch that is perfect for brick house portraits. It is also a great way to add woven details. I suggest using the entire six strands of floss.

1 Create a row of backstitches.

2 Start a new row above the row in Step 1, beginning on the right. Make a back stitch half the length of the back stitch below it.

3 Create another back stitch, this time the same length as the stitches in the Step 1 row. Continue backstitching, creating a second row that is staggered/offset from the first row.

4 Starting at the left side of your stitch area and working right, make a third row that is staggered/offset from the second row. Stitch this row the same as the first row.

5 Repeat Steps 2–4, alternating stitching right to left and left to right, staggering each row from the previous one.

Fly Stitch

Fly stitch is perfect for capturing organic, curved shapes. It is often used to create foliage, feathers and even fur.

1 Create a straight stitch, but do not pull the thread all the way through.

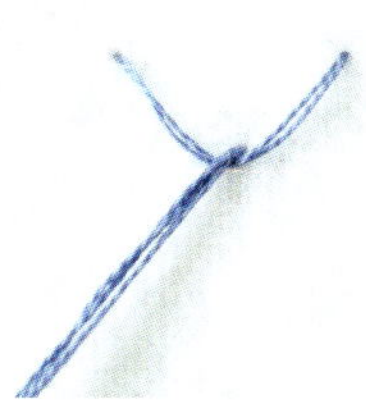

2 Center the needle in the middle of the stitch. Bring it up about ¼″ below the straight stitch, passing the needle through the loop of the loose straight stitch. Pull taut.

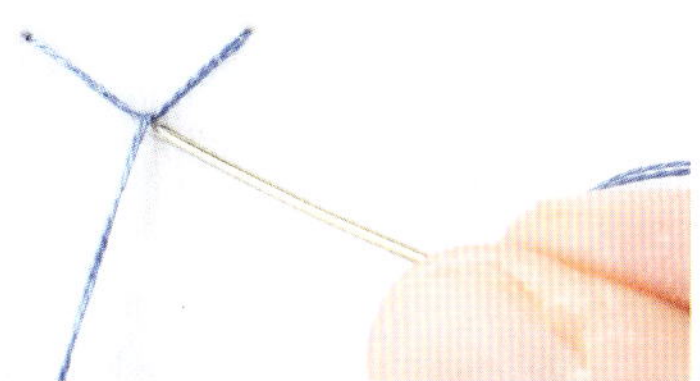

3 Bring the needle over the straight stitch and back down through the hole you came up in Step 2. Pull tight.

***TIP:** You can vary the size of this stitch by changing the length of the first straight stitch or by modifying the placement of the anchoring stitch.*

stitching text

DOES MY PROJECT NEED TEXT?

Ask yourself:

- Will text be distracting to the overall piece or will it blend with what is already there?
- Will text enhance the mood and aesthetic you are trying to achieve?
- Will the text clutter the piece or is there space for it?

Text with names and dates can be great for a nostalgic piece, providing context to a portrait or event. It's also important to consider the style. Don't feel pressured to fill every empty space on a piece—it's okay to leave breathing room!

CHOOSING FONT

If you have decided to add text to a project, you can ask yourself many of the same questions when it comes to choosing font. Make sure it matches the mood, style, and subject matter of the piece. For example, if you are working on a bright, bold piece, consider a font that's thicker and made up of rigid lines. A project that is more delicate might call for a font with thinner, curvier lines.

Handwriting

Digital font

TRANSFERRING FONT

If you wish to create text using your own handwriting, you can easily write directly onto light colored felt with a Frixion pen. If you are trying to transfer someone else's handwritten text, such as a signature or special note, trace over the writing using a piece of tracing paper or wash-away paper (see Transferring Templates, page 19).

Using a digital font is also an easy way to add text to a project. Simply type up what you wish to add to your project and print directly onto wash-away paper.

COMPOSING FONT

Onto Background

In some cases, it makes visual sense to add text directly to your project's background. This might work if you have a lot of negative space that needs filling or if you want to incorporate the text as an integral part of the subject itself.

Text Banner

Another option for adding text to a project is to create a separate banner, tag, or felt plaque. This is a wonderful option if you are keeping a project in its original hoop but want to cover the clasp. It is also a great way to add three-dimensionality to a frame.

TIP: *If you are unsure about adding text to a piece, a text banner is a good option to try, as you can move the text around and play with composition before committing.*

Riehle Home
1976
Milly

hoop backing

I like to think of a hoop back as a secret keeper of time. It reflects the number of times you switched your thread color, how often you got a knot in your floss, and the times you decided to backtrack with your needle. You may choose to leave your hoop back uncovered to marvel at the "mess" behind the beauty. Or, you may wish to hide the back for a polished look. Either way, there are a few ways to ensure the back of your project is finished properly.

FELT BACKING

Tighten the felt in your hoop by pulling on the excess and cinching the clasp at the top. Then, trim any excess felt down to ⅛″ around the entire hoop.

Blanket Stitching

Blanket stitching a backing onto the hoop is my preferred method for finishing. Use a sheet of felt that is the same color as the front of the hoop. Trace around the outside of the inner hoop with a marking pen or pencil, then cut out the circle and remove any marks. Lay the felt circle over the hoop back so the perimeter lines up with the lip of excess felt.

Bring the needle up between the lip of the felt and the circle so that the knot is hidden between them. Blanket stitch the edge of the felt circle and the trimmed excess felt (see Blanket Stitch, page 29) all the way around the hoop.

GLUING

If you wish to simply leave the back uncovered or want to glue on decorative paper as a backing, trim the excess felt down even further, so that it is nearly flush with the hoop.

Trace and cut a paper circle the size of the outer edge of the inside ring of the hoop. If desired, decorate the paper backing.

Run a line of hot glue along the trimmed felt edge on the back of the hoop. Line the paper up with the glue ring, and press firmly. If you prefer to use E6000 glue instead of hot glue, allow up to 24 hrs for glue to cure fully.

NOTE: *While covering the back of the hoop can simply be an aesthetic choice to hide all of your stitching and knots, it can also be an opportunity to include little sentimental details. A small pocket on the back could include a note, business card, or small keepsake such as pet hair.*

designing your own project

While this book includes 10 projects you can follow step-by-step, you may wish to stitch your own house, pet, or nature-inspired portrait. The process can seem daunting at first, but after reading these tips and practicing the many skills and methods of portraiture in this book, you'll be ready to tackle your own project with ease and confidence.

INSPIRATION

Your subject matter can sometimes be quite obvious—you may have a family home you wish to recreate, or a beloved pet you want to memorialize. But other times, inspiration can be more elusive. I find taking a long walk and getting outside to be the best way to brainstorm for project ideas. After all, nature offers up the most beautiful and unique inspiration. Doing a mundane chore like washing dishes or folding laundry, is another great way to come up with new ideas. While your body is physically busy, your mind is free to wander and imagine.

WORKING FROM A PHOTO

Many portraits are created from photos because they are easy to work with. Subjects are frozen in time which means not having to worry about changes in position, lighting or color. If you are basing your project off of a photograph, it is important that you have a high-quality image to work from. If the photo is a digital file, be sure that you can zoom in without the image becoming too pixelated. Additionally, make sure the photo's colors are accurate to the subject.

Creating a Template

Visualize your subject as a series of levels, working background to foreground and breaking things down into layers.

Pet reference photo provided by Katie Davidson

House reference photo provided by Joanna Weingartner

1 Trace the photo using tracing vellum and a felt tip marker. Be sure to outline important details and features of the subject.

2 Using a lightbox or window, trace isolated shapes from the drawing onto freezer paper. Decide which pieces need to be in the back (and therefore larger), and which need to be in the front (and therefore smaller).

3 Iron the freezer paper templates from Step 2 onto their coordinating felt colors.

4 Cut around the freezer paper templates.

5 Peel the freezer paper from the felt. These felt layers are ready to be stitched!

WORKING FROM A SKETCH

There are several reasons you might choose to work from a sketch rather than directly from a photo. This allows you to create a portrait in your own artistic style. Or, you simply may not have a single photograph that works perfectly as a reference, so you may need to combine or edit what you have. Whatever the reason, create a drawing to work from, then follow the same steps for Creating a Template (page 42).

CHOOSING BACKGROUND AND COMPOSITION

Deciding on a background is up to personal preference. But, there are several things to ask yourself: Do you want the subject to be the main focus and have space to breathe? Do you want a detailed background to give more context and meaning to the portrait? Do you want to have an opportunity to use color in an otherwise drab portrait? See Creating a Background (page 19) for more.

Beach Bungalow

FINISHED PROJECT: 6½″ × 7″

My friend's cheery home, bursting with flowers and personality, is the perfect project for mastering the fundamentals of felt portraiture. While this piece introduces important felt appliqué basics, it's the embroidery details that truly bring it to life. The tiny octagonal window is a nod to historical New England housing, while the unique fish ornament and porch bench add warm, coastal charm. Finish off the piece with the vibrant blooms of the garden, and the result is a cozy beach bungalow that you wish you could escape to!

MATERIALS

6" embroidery hoop
Sizes 8, 6, and 3 embroidery needles
Fiskars Micro-Tip Scissors
Beach Bungalow Templates (page 15)
Quilter's Freezer Paper Sheets
Iron

THREAD AND FELT

1 sheet 12″ × 18″ Linen felt
1 sheet 9″ × 12″ Pewter felt
1 sheet 9″ × 12″ Red felt
1 sheet 9″ × 12″ Graphite felt
1 sheet 9″ × 12″ Black felt
1 sheet 9″ × 12″ White felt
1 sheet 9″ × 12″ Morel Bellwether felt
1 sheet 9″ × 12″ Ash felt
1 sheet 9″ × 12″ Lunar Bellwether felt

DMC six-stranded cotton embroidery floss (1 skein of each)

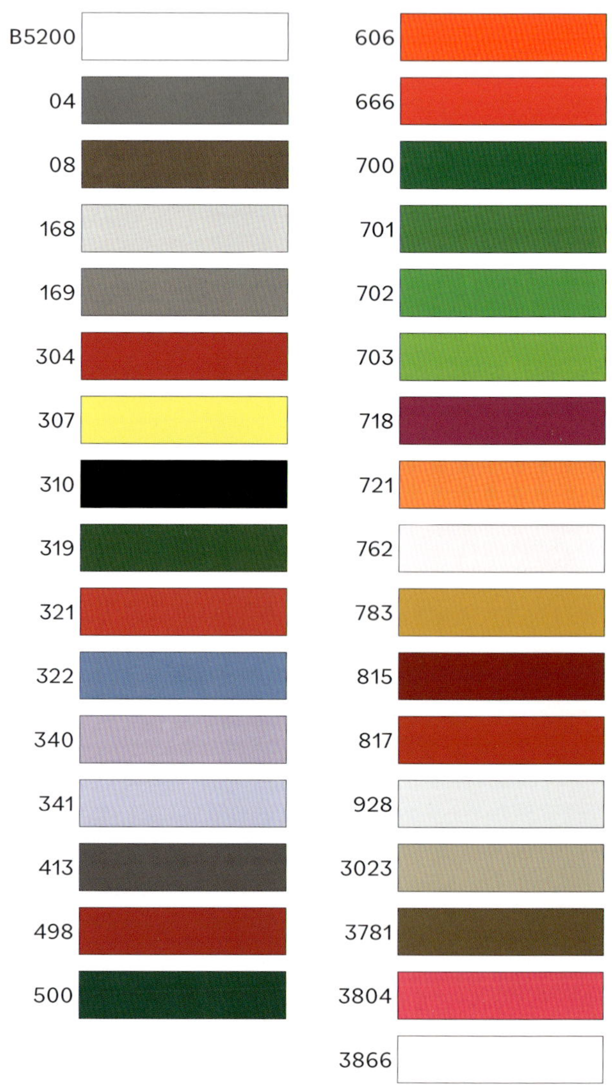

Cut felt pieces for Beach Bungalow

CUT LIST

Transfer the Beach Bungalow Templates to the felt using freezer paper, and then cut them out as directed below (see Transferring Templates, page 11). This portrait contains very small pieces so I suggest using freezer paper instead of a Frixion pen. Do not cut along notches or dotted lines, as these are placement guides. Make sure every piece is labeled.

Cut felt pieces for Beach Bungalow, layered

Background & Backing

Cut 1 circle 7″ diameter from Linen felt (background).

Cut 1 circle 6¼″ diameter from Linen felt (hoop backing).

House

Cut 1 Template B1, B5, B9, B14 and B17 from Pewter felt.

Cut 2 Templates B20 from Pewter felt.

Cut 1 Template B24 from Black felt.

Cut 2 Templates B2 from Ash felt.

Cut 1 Template B3 and B19 from Lunar Bellwether felt.

Cut 1 Template B4, B8 and B13 from White felt.

Cut 2 Templates B10 and B22 from White felt.

Cut 1 Template B6, B7, B11, B12 and B16 from Graphite felt.

Cut 1 Template B15 and B18 from Morel Bellwether felt.

Cut 1 Template B21 from Red felt.

PREPARE THE HOOP

Place and tighten the 7″ Linen felt circle into the 6″ beechwood hoop.

FELT APPLIQUÉ

For this section, use a size 8 needle and 1 strand of thread. Unless otherwise specified, attach each piece with a running stitch around the perimeter, leaving a ¹⁄₁₆″ seam allowance.

1 Place H1 in the center of the hoop, and stitch with 168. Affix 1 B2 piece to the bottom corner of the B1 piece with 169, matching notches. Position B3 over the double notches on the left side of the roof. Use 928 to running stitch up the center, and add 1 straight stitch across the top. Position 1 B10 piece over the double notches in the middle of the roof. Affix with 1 straight stitch of DMC B5200 in the center.

2 Attach B5 with 168 and a running stitch up the center (see template B1 for placement). Affix B6 and B7 with 413 (see template B1 for placement). Layer B8 at the bottom of B7 and running stitch through the center with DMC B5200.

3 Layer B9 over B1, aligning it on the left hand side. Attach using 168. Place the other B2 piece over the first B2 piece in Step 1. Affix using 169. Layer the other B10 piece over the existing right chimney. Attach with 1 straight stitch of DMC B5200 in the center.

4 Attach B11 and B12 with 413 (refer to template B9 for placement). Running stitch through the center of B14 with 168 (refer to template B9 for placement). Layer B13 along the bottom of B11 and running stitch through the center with DMC B5200. Layer B4 over the right chimney, matching up notches in template. Make 2 straight stitches on both sides with DMC B5200. Place B15 over the top half of the chimney, and attach with 4 straight stitches of 08 on each side.

5 Layer B16 over the main roof area of B9. Attach using 413.

6 Align B17 just below the roof line (B16). Attach with 168. Position B18 to the right of B2 and along the bottom of the house, matching notches. Attach with 08.

7 Align 1 B20 piece along the left side of B17. Place the other on the right so that it overlaps the sliding door (B12) slightly. Running stitch through the center of each with 168. Align B19 at the top of B17. Running stitch along the middle with 928. Affix B21 with 321 and stitch B22 pieces on either side with DMC B5200. Attach both B23 pieces with 413 (refer to template B17 for placement). Then affix B24 below the apex of the roof using 2 straight stitches of 310.

8 Place B25 over B19, aligning the top edges. Running stitch through the center with DMC B5200. Position B26 along the bottom of the porch (B18). Running stitch through the middle with 08. Place both B27 pieces at the base of the door windows (B22). Secure with 2 straight stitches of DMC B5200.

EMBROIDERY

For this section, I suggest using needles with larger eyes. A size 6 needle will work for most of the steps, but when using more than 3 strands of thread, switch to a size 3 needle. Refer to the stitch library (page 26) for step-by-step instructions for each embroidery stitch used in this project.

Architectural Detail

SIDING

To create the appearance of siding, use 1 strand of 169 and make long straight stitches across the Pewter felt pieces. Space the stitches about ¹⁄₁₆″ apart, stopping and starting on each side of window, door and corner details.

WINDOWS, DOOR AND FINISHING TOUCHES

1 Use 3 strands of DMC B5200. Outline both main windows (B23) with a back stitch along each edge. Divide each window in half with 2 satin stitches. Split the sliding door into thirds with 2 long, vertical straight stitches. Add 2 satin stitches on the right side of the sliding door. Finally, use 2 backstitches to outline the bottom and right side of the far right window (B6). Add 2 satin stitches to divide the window in half.

2 Stitch 8 evenly-spaced squares, each made of 4 back stitches, on the main door (B21) using 1 strand of 815. Directly under the top stitch of each square, make a straight stitch with 1 strand of 817. Use 2 strands of 815 to outline the door's perimeter with 4 back stitches. Use 1 strand of 783 to stitch a French knot half way down the left hand side of the door. Make a French knot just below that using 2 strands of 783.

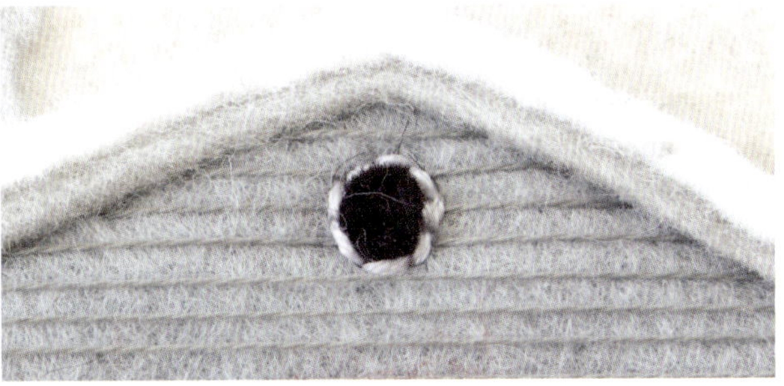

3 Outline the octagonal window (B24) with a backstitch in 3 strands of DMC B5200.

4 Use 3 strands of DMC B5200 to backstitch the perimeter of the main door (1stitch per side). Use 2 strands of 513 to make 4 satin stitches in the center of each panel on the sides of the door (B22). Make stitches about ⅝″ long, extending down to the flower pots. Use 1 strand of DMC B5200 to make 4 horizontal straight stitches across each section of satin stitches. Use 2 stands of DMC B5200 to outline the satin stitches with long back stitches.

5 Use 2 strands of 169. Add another layer of outlines around both main windows, the top of the main door, the windows on the side of the door, and the far right window with long back stitches. Outline the octagonal window with another layer of backstitches. Add a single vertical straight stitch to the center of the main windows, centered on the white satin stitches. Add a vertical straight stitch on the right edge of the sliding door. Make 1 vertical straight stitch in the middle of the 2 satin stitches on the far right window.

6 Make 2 long straight stitches along the bottom of the roof line using 2 strands of 169. To create a flood light, make 2 French knots with 413, between the main door and octagonal window. Add 2 tiny satin stitches below and between the knots with 2 strands of 413.

PORCH RAILING

1 Use 3 strands of DMC B5200 to make 2 long parallel straight stitches that span from the center of the sliding door to the running stitches on the right edge of the house. Then, use 2 strands of the same color to make vertical straight stitches between the parallel railings, spacing them about $\frac{1}{16}$″ apart.

2 Stitch 4 posts about ½″ apart with 6 strands of DMC B5200 and vertical straight stitches. Use 4 strands of the same color to make tiny horizontal straight stitches on the top of each post.

Decor

PORCH BENCH

1 Create the porch bench under the right window. Use 3 strands of DMC B5200 to make 3 horizontal satin stitches about ¼″ long. Switch to 2 strands of the same color, and add 2 straight vertical stitches about ⅛″ long. Add 2 more horizontal stitches to create a rectangle, then satin stitch slats into the rectangle.

2 Use 2 strands of DMC B5200 to make 4 vertical straight stitches for the legs of the bench. Add 2 diagonal straight stitches for the arm rests.

POTTED PLANTS

1 Straight stitch a horizontal band on each pot with 2 strands of 762. Use 3 strands of 319 to make tall clusters of seed stitches coming up from the pots and covering half the windows. Sprinkle French knots among the seed stitches with 1 strand of 498.

2 Make 5 new pots for the porch with horizontal satin stitching. Using 2 strands of each color, make a 310 rectangle on the left side of the porch, 3 top-hat-shaped-pots in 3781 on either side of the porch and below the bench, and a tall, egg-shaped pot in 322.

3 Top the 3 brown pots with French knots using 2 strands of 700. Add overlapping straight stitches in 2 strands of 702 in the remaining 2 pots.

4 To make flowers, add 6 French knots to each brown pot, 3 knots using 1 strand of 606 and 3 knots using 1 strand of 718. Using 1 strand of 721, make 5 single cross stitches on top of the black pot foliage. Repeat for the blue pot using 1 strand of 307.

FLOWERS

1 Starting next to the blue pot, make a cluster of French knots using 2 strands of 500. Sprinkle in red flowers by making 8 French knots using 3 strands of 304. In the center of each red flower, use 1 strand of 307 to make a tiny straight stitch.

2 Use 2 strands of 701 and make 3 satin stitches slanting left and 3 more slanting right. Make 2 vertical straight stitches coming up from the satin stitches, and then top them with 1-strand French knots of 307.

3 Below the third railing post from the left, use 3 strands of 702 to make a large cluster of French knots. Make 3 clusters of 4 French knots using 1 strand of 340. Repeat using 1 strand of 341.

4 On either side of the Step 3 flowers, add straight stitches of varying lengths using 2 strands of 703. Add flowers along the stems by stitching French knots with 1 strand of DMC B5200 and then 3804.

5 To create a trellis above the porch railing, use 2 strands 3781 and make one long straight stitch in the middle of the siding corner (B14). Switch to 1 strand of 3781, and create 4 small perpendicular straight stitches along the previous stitch. Use 1 strand of 701 and a stem stitch to make a vine that winds through the trellis. Add French knot flowers with 1 strand of 371.

6 Starting alongside the bottom right of the house, use 1 strand of 700 to make a tall cluster of French knots that extend up the side of the house. Switch to 2 strands of 666 to sprinkle in French knot flowers.

FISH ORNAMENT

Use 2 strands of 3023 and a satin stitch to create a simple fish shape on the left side of the house. Outline the fish with a back stitch using 1 strand of 04.

GRASS

Using 1 strand of 702 and 1 strand of 703, make criss-crossing straight stitches to create grass in the empty space in front of the house and between the brown pots.

DISPLAY

Use the 6¼″ Linen felt circle and DMC 3866 to back the hoop (see Hoop Backing, page 38). While you can certainly frame this piece, its simplicity and negative space make it a good candidate for leaving unframed. Simply hang the portrait on a hook or nail using the clasp at the top of the hoop.

Riehle Family Home

FINISHED PROJECT: 8¾″ × 8¾″

A friend's childhood home nestles peacefully on a hill in this commemorative portrait. Much like an heirloom quilt, this project is pieced together through a compilation of nostalgic details and memories from years past. Take a deeper dive into the layering process with this portrait, working the entire surface area for a full landscape effect. Use various stitches like the French knot and brick stitch to create life-like textures, and discover how text can add significance to a piece.

MATERIALS

6" embroidery hoop
Sizes 8, 6, and 3 embroidery needles
Fiskars Micro-Tip Scissors
Riehle Family Home Templates (page 15)
Quilter's Freezer Paper Sheets
Frixion Heat Erasable Pen
Wash-away stabilizer transfer paper
Tombow ABT Pro Art Marker P977
Iron
Modern Hoopla Circle Frame (carmel finish)

THREAD AND FELT

1 sheet 12″ × 18″ Sky felt
1 sheet 9″ × 12″ Willow Bellwether felt
1 sheet 9″ × 12″ Nori Bellwether felt
1 sheet 9″ × 12″ Zucchini felt
1 sheet 9″ × 12″ Sherwood Bellwether felt
1 sheet 9″ × 12″ Nutmeg felt
1 sheet 9″ × 12″ Graphite felt
1 sheet 9″ × 12″ Ash felt
1 sheet 9″ × 12″ Cinnamon felt
1 sheet 9″ × 12″ Lunar Bellwether felt

DMC six-stranded cotton embroidery floss (1 skein of each)

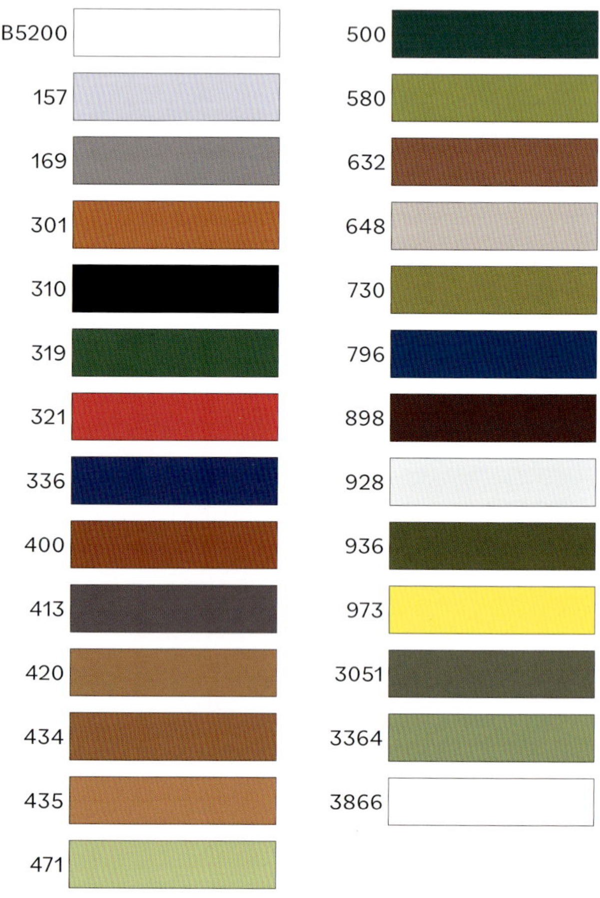

Riehle Home
1976

House reference photo provided by Joanna Weingartner

Cut felt pieces for background

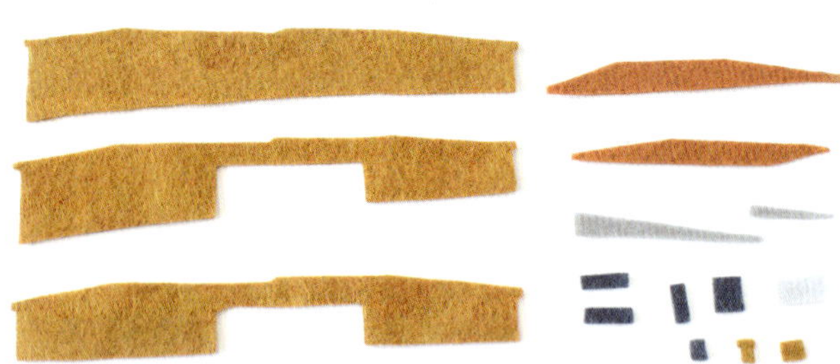
Cut felt pieces for house of Riehle Family Home

Cut felt pieces for Riehle Family Home, layered

CUT LIST

Transfer the Riehle Family Home Templates to the felt using freezer paper and cut them out as directed below (see Transferring Templates, page 19). This portrait contains very small pieces so I suggest using freezer paper as opposed to a Frixion pen. Do not cut along notches or dotted lines, as these are placement guides. Make sure every piece is labeled.

Background & Backing

Cut 1 circle 7″ diameter from Sky felt (background).

Cut 1 circle 6¼″ diameter from Sky felt (hoop backing).

Landscaping

Cut 1 Template R1 from Willow Bellwether felt.

Cut 1 Template R2 and R5 from Nori Bellwether felt.

Cut 1 Template R3 and R4 from Zucchini felt.

Cut 1 Template R6 from Sherwood Bellwether felt.

House

Cut 1 Template R7, R8, R9, R10 and R14 from Nutmeg felt.

Cut 1 Template R9, R12, and R13 from Graphite felt.

Cut 2 Templates R18 from Graphite felt.

Cut 1 Template R11 and R15 from Ash felt.

Cut 1 Template R16 and R17 from Cinnamon felt.

Cut 1 Template R19 from Lunar felt.

PREPARE THE BACKGROUND

Use a size 8 needle. Refer to the stitch library (page 26) for step-by-step instructions for each embroidery stitch used in this project.

1 Use a blanket appliqué stitch with 1 strand of 471 along the top of R1 to attach it to the bottom of the 6¼″ Sky felt circle. Space the stitches about 3⁄16″ apart. Pre-soak this unit to prepare it for wash-away paper. Allow the felt to dry.

2 Put the background from Step 1 in the hoop and tighten the clasp. Use a Frixion pen to mark the perimeter of the inside of the hoop ring. Remove the background from the hoop.

FELT APPLIQUÉ

During the felt appliqué process, use 1 strand of embroidery floss and a size 8 needle. Unless otherwise noted, running stitch around the perimeter of each piece leaving a 1⁄16″ seam allowance.

Background Landscaping

These pieces are stitched outside of the hoop so their edges will be perfectly aligned with the hoop.

1 Using the Frixion pen marks and R1 as guidelines, line up R2, R3 and R7. Attach R2 with 936, R3 with 730, and R7 with 434.

2 Position R5 over R3 and attach with 936. Layer R4 over R2 and stitch with 730.

3 Place R6 over R4 and attach with 500. Use an iron to erase the Frixion pen marks. Put the felt unit into the hoop, and tighten.

House

1 Overlap R8 over R7 slightly, aligning with the double notches on the left side of the roof. Attach with 434 and 2 perpendicular straight stitches. Overlap Nutmeg R9 over R7 slightly, aligning with the double notches on the right side of the roof. Make 4 straight stitches on each side with 434. Layer R10 over R7 and affix with 434.

2 Position Graphite R9, R11, R12 and R13 (refer to template for placement). Make 1 straight stitch on each side of R9 with 413. Running stitch R12 and R13 around the perimeter with 413. Running stitch through the center of R11 with 169.

3 Place R14 over R10 and attach with 434. Align R16 in the upper left corner of R14 and attach with 301. Align R17 in the upper right corner of R14 and affix with 301. Position both R18 pieces below the left roof and attach with 413. Layer R15 below the left side of the house and stitch down with 169. Place R19 below the right roof and attach with 928.

EMBROIDERY

For this section, I suggest using needles with larger eyes. A size 6 needle will work for most of the steps, but when using more than 3 strands of thread, switch to a size 3 needle.

Architectural Detail

ROOF, WINDOWS, DOOR AND PORCH

1 Make a long straight stitch under the roof on either side of the house with 5 strands of 3364.

2 Use 2 strands of 3364. Outline the left and right sides of all of the windows with straight stitches. Add a straight stitch along the top of the smallest window (R9). Add 2 satin stitches in the middle of each long window on the left. Make 2 horizontal straight stitches across the middle window (R12) dividing it into 3 equal sections. Then make 1 vertical straight stitch to divide the window into 6 rectangles. Make 2 vertical stitches on the largest window (R19) to divide it into 9 rectangles.

3 Make straight stitches along the bottom of all of the windows using 3 strands of 648.

4 Use 3 strands of 648. Make 1 straight stitch across the middle of the door (R13). Make 2 long straight stitches along the right side of the door. On the lower half of the door, use a horizontal satin stitch to fill half of the rectangle.

5 Make straight stitches with 1 strand of 413 at the top and right side of each rectangle within the largest window.

6 Make 1 long straight stitch above each green roof line and along the middle roof section with 3 strands of 413. Above this, with 4 strands of 3866, make 1 long straight stitch along the left roof line and 1 spanning the rest of the roof line.

7 Make 3 vertical straight stitches for porch posts using 3 strands of 435. Place one to the left of the door, one in the center of the middle window, and one on the left hand side of the small window. Switch to 4 strands of 169 and create a straight stitch from the end of the stoop (R11) to the right side of the porch.

BRICK

1 Using a dispersed variation of a brick stitch and 2 strands of 435, make staggered straight stitches on the left and right sides of the house. Switch to 1 strand of 435 and brick stitch within the porch area.

2 Repeat Step 1 using 2 strands of 400, 632 and 898 for the left and right sides of the house. Use 1 strand of each color for the porch area.

3 Use the Tombow marker to lightly shade the porch area. Avoid shading the windows, the door and the stoop.

LAMPPOST, ROOF VENT, AND FLAG POLE

1 At the base of the left side of the house, make a single straight stitch, about ½″ long, using 2 strands of 310. Above this, make a small perpendicular line about ⅛″ long. With 1 strand of 310, make 2 diagonal straight stitches that connect the first stitch to the perpendicular stitch. Make a French knot on top of the perpendicular stitch. Use 1 strand of 648 to make a French knot inside the triangular area.

Lampost: Circles represent French knots

2 Create a small roof vent on the main roof area, above the small window. Make 2 tiny satin stitches with 2 strands of 898. With 1 strand of DMC B5200, make a small straight stitch at the base of the satin stitches.

3 Make a 1½″ vertical straight stitch with 4 strands of 3866 on the left hand side of the house between the small and largest window. Place a French knot on the top using 1 strand of 420.

4 Use 2 strands of thread to make the American flag. At the top left side of the flagpole, make a triangle of satin stitches with 336. Along the base of the triangle, make a horizontal straight stitch with DMC B5200. Below that, make a slightly longer straight stitch with 321. Repeat this once more, making each stitch longer than the one before. Below the final red stitch, make 5 vertical straight stitches. Start with 321 and alternate with DMC B5200.

336
B5200
321
B5200
321
321 B5200 321 B5200 321

American Flag color diagram

5 Create an Air Force flag directly under the American flag, using 2 strands of 796 and a satin stitch. Use 1 strand 973 and stem stitch a half circle in the middle of the flag.

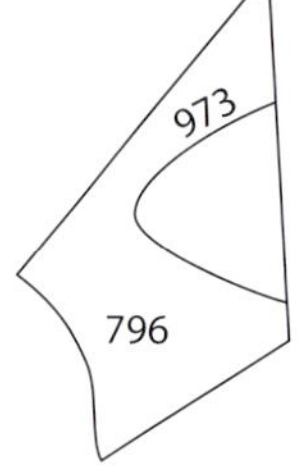

Air Force Flag color diagram

Landscaping

BUSHES

1 Make clusters of French knots using 2 strands of 319 as shown by the Bush Placement Diagram.

Bush Placement Diagram

NOTE: *It may seem counterproductive to embroider house details and then stitch over them with landscaping. However, I find it looks more realistic to work each layer fully so they have uniform thickness and protrude evenly.*

2 Make remaining bushes (shown in black) with clusters of French knots using 2 strands of 3051.

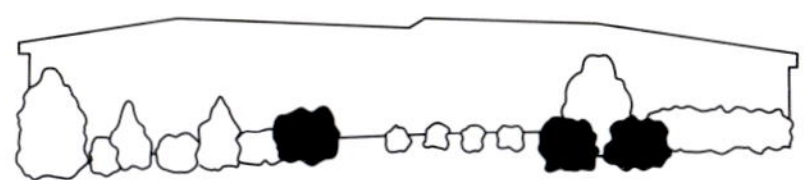

Bush Placement Diagram

GRASS

1 Using 1 strand of 471, make vertical straight stitches of varying lengths across the lawn. Make the stitches nearest to the house short and close together. Make the stitches longer and more spread out as you move away from the house towards the hoop edge.

2 Repeat Step 1 using 1 strand of 580.

Text

1 Print Riehle Family Home Text Template onto the wash-away paper. Peel and stick over the lawn (see Transferring Templates, page 19).

2 Stitch over the serifs of text using 1 strand of 3866. Make straight stitches over straight serifs and stem stitching on curved serifs. Fill in the rest of the font with horizontal satin stitches of 2 strands of 3866.

3 Take the finished piece out of the hoop, and gently rinse away the paper. Wet only the bottom half of the project, as the rest was not pre-soaked. Allow it to dry before returning it into the hoop.

4 Outline the left side of the text with 2 strands of 319. Straight stitch along the straight letters, and back stitch along the curved letters.

FRAME/DISPLAY

Use the 6 ¼" Sky felt circle and DMC 157 to back the hoop (see Hoop Backing, page 38). Place the hoop inside the Modern Hoopla frame. Your project is ready to hang on the wall and enjoy!

Riehle Home
1976

Edwin Dog Portrait

FINISHED PROJECT: 8¾″ × 8¾″

Edwin was more than a pet, he was a soul pup, best friend, and constant companion. His energy and character could not be contained in the confines of a two dimensional photo—which is why he deserved a non-traditional portrait, a feat of fiber engineering, with 15 layers of felt and multiple levels of thread painting. This portrait not only tests the limits of felt appliqué, it explores the use of various stitches to achieve striking textures and details.

MATERIALS

6" embroidery hoop
Sizes 8, 6, and 3 embroidery needles
Fiskars Micro-Tip Scissors
Edwin Dog Templates (page 15)
Quilter's Freezer Paper Sheets
Frixion Heat Erasable Pen
Iron
Tombow ABT Pro PN29
White water soluble pencil
Stiffy Fabric Stiffener
Wax paper
Paintbrush
Pliers (optional)
Modern Hoopla Circle Frame (black finish)

THREAD AND FELT

1 sheet 12″ × 18″ Blue Spruce felt
1 sheet 9″ × 12″ Slate Bellwether felt
1 sheet 9″ × 12″ Parchment felt
1 sheet 9″ × 12″ Ash Bellwether felt
1 sheet 9″ × 12″ Smoke felt
1 sheet 9″ × 12″ Black felt
1 sheet 9″ × 12″ White felt
1 sheet 9″ × 12″ Lunar Bellwether felt
1 sheet 9″ × 12″ Hazelnut Bellwether felt

DMC six-stranded cotton embroidery floss (1 skein of each)

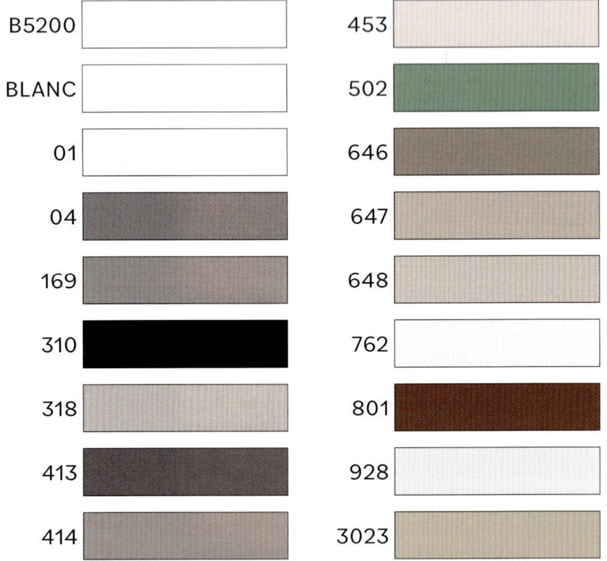

"I truly believe the love of my life came in the form of a dog named Edwin." — Katie Davidson, Edwin's owner

Pet reference photo provided by Katie Davidson

Cut felt pieces for Edwin

Layered felt pieces for Edwin

CUT LIST

Transfer the Edwin Dog Templates to the felt using freezer paper and cut them out as directed below (see Transferring Templates, page 19). I do not recommend using a Frixion pen for transferring these templates because many of the pieces are small and cut from dark felt. Do not cut along dotted lines, as these are placement guides. Make sure each piece is labeled.

Background & Backing

Cut 1 circle 7″ diameter from Blue Spruce felt (background).

Cut 1 circle 6¼″ diameter from Blue Spruce felt (hoop backing).

Edwin

Cut 1 Template E1, E3 and E20 from Slate Bellwether felt.

Cut 1 Template E2, E5, E6, E7, E11, E12, E15, E16 and E21 from Parchment felt.

Cut 1 Template E4, E8, E25 and E27 from Ash felt.

Cut 1 Template E9, E10 and E24 from Smoke felt.

Cut 1 Template E13, E14, E17, E18, E28, E29, E30 and E31 from Black felt.

Cut 1 Template E23 and E26 from White felt.

Cut 1 Template E19 and E22 from Lunar Bellwether felt.

Cut 1 Template E32 and E33 from Hazelnut felt.

PREPARE THE HOOP

Place and tighten the 7″ Blue Spruce felt circle into the 6″ embroidery hoop.

FELT APPLIQUÉ

During the felt appliqué process, use 1 strand of embroidery floss and a size 8 needle. Unless otherwise specified, use a running stitch around the perimeter of each piece, leaving about a 1⁄16″ seam allowance.

1 Position E1 in the middle of the hoop, and stitch with 413. Layer E2 over the far left paw, and attach with 762.

2 Place E3 over E1, matching edges, and affix with 413.

3 Layer E4 over E3, matching edges, and stitch with 169. Position E5 over the middle paw and E6 over the right paw. Attach both with 762.

4 Place E7 over E4, matching the edges, and stitch down with 762. Layer E8 over E7 the same way, and attach with 169. Finally, layer E9 over E8, and attach with 318.

5 Layer E10 over E9, and stitch with 318. Position E11 along the bottom right of E10, and attach with 762.

6 Place E12 over E10, and attach with 762. Layer E13 on the left ear and E14 on the right ear, matching notches (refer to template for placement). Stitch with 310.

7 Layer E15 and E16 over E12, aligning the edges. Attach with 762.

8 Position E18 over the left ear and E17 over the right ear, matching the curves. Attach with 310. Make 1 line of running stitches up the center of the thin sections, and stitch around the perimeter of the wider parts at the top.

9 Layer E19 over E15. Attach with 928.

10 Layer E20 over E19, matching the bottom edges of the chin. Attach with 413.

11 Position E21 over E20, again matching the chins. Attach with 762.

12 Place E22 along the bottom of E21, again matching the chins. Attach with 928.

13 Layer E23 along the bottom of E22, matching the chins. Attach with DMC B5200. Position E24 centered right above E23, and stitch with 318. Place E25 close to the bottom of E23, and attach with 169 (refer to template E23 for placement).

14 Place E26 over E23, lining it up with E24. Stitch with DMC B5200. Position E27 at the bottom of E26, directly in the middle on the small divot. Stitch with 169.

15 Layer E28 between E24 and E27. Attach with 310. Position E29 over E28, and affix with 310.

16 Position E30 on the upper left side of E21. Make 3 small straight stitches around the outside edge with 310. Repeat for E31, placing on the upper right side. Layer E32 inside of E30 and E33 inside of E31. Make 2 small straight stitches in the center of each with 801.

EMBROIDERY

For this section, use needles with larger eyes. A size 6 needle will work for most of the steps, but when using more than 3 strands of thread or stitching through more than 7 layers of felt, switch to a size 3 needle. Refer to the stitch library (page 26) for step-by-step instructions for each embroidery stitch used in this project.

TIP: *Cut the thread longer than usual when stitching through so many layers of felt. This will help you avoid having to re-thread your needle as often.*

A Method to the Madness

It may seem pointless to go through the work of meticulously cutting and stitching layers of different colored felt, only to go back and cover most of it up with embroidery. However, I always follow this method for portraiture. It gives you the option of creating a more simple portrait, with little to no embroidery. The layering of specific felt colors can stand alone in making the project look lifelike if preferred. If I decide to embroider lots of details, the felt layers act as a guideline. It's almost like my version of coloring—or stitching—by number.

I prefer to be thorough with felt appliqué because every project has at least one layer where the felt will show through under the embroidery, which gives the project texture variety. For example, while a dog's body may be heavily stitched to give the texture of fur, the tongue or eyes may be left almost entirely unstitched to convey a more smooth texture.

Body

LEGS

1 Use 1 strand of 310 to make French knot toenails at the ends of each paw. Add 4 to the left and middle paws, and 3 to the right. Use 1 strand of 413 to straight stitch toes between the knots.

2 Make tiny clusters of seed stitches with 1 strand of 646 to add spots to the paws.

3 On the furthest back leg haunch, use 1 strand of 646 to make long and short stitches radiating out from the body. Space the stitches so that some of the felt shows through. On the leg, angle the stitches down towards the paw. Long and short stitch another layer with 1 strand of 413. Make a straight stitch between the leg and haunch (E1 and E3) using 1 strand of 310.

4 Use 1 strand of 646. Create 2 staggered satin stitches on the right side of the middle leg. Make 2 satin stitches on the left side of the right leg. Then make slanted straight stitches that wrap around the left side of the middle leg and the right side of the right leg.

5 Make tiny seed stitches with 1 strand of 648 above the middle and right paws. Make several upward slanting straight stitches on the middle leg, left of the satin stitches. Repeat on the right leg on both sides of the satin stitches.

***NOTE:** Your stitching may seem haphazard or even a bit chaotic at this stage. Remember that changing stitch length, direction, thickness, and color all helps make your portrait look more realistic. After all, nothing in nature is uniform in color, size, or texture!*

CHEST

1 Fill in the lowest layer of the chest with long and short stitches using 2 strands of DMC BLANC and 2 strands of 648. Stagger the strands of 648 over the middle leg and to the left of the right leg.

2 On the next layer of the chest, starting on the right side, use 1 strand of 169 to make straight stitches that overlap and crisscross. Layer in straight stitches with 1 strand of 3023. Switch to 2 strands of 3023 and use a long and short stitch on the left side. Sprinkle clusters of straight stitches between them, using 1 strand of 413. Leave gaps as shown.

3 Continue filling in the same layer, starting with the left side up around the side of the dog. Using a long and short stitch and 2 strands of 413, create two large spots, one at the upper edge (alongside E3) and the other below it (alongside E9). Use 2 strands of 647 to fill the area between those spots with long and short stitches. Use 2 strands of 453 to make long and short stitches in between the Step 2 stitches in 3023.

4 Long and short stitch with 1 strand of 310 on the edges of both large 413 patches. Sprinkle in a few tiny straight stitches along the small spots in 413 and along the right side. Use 2 strands of 414 to long and short stitch above around the Step 2 stitches in 169. Use 1 strand of 413 to long and short stitch the 414 stitches. Use 2 strands of 310 to finish filling the right side with long and short stitches slanted towards the nose.

5 Use 1 strand of 647 to long and short stitch across the next layers of the chest (in Smoke felt). Leave spaces between stitches and angle them in a fan-like pattern Add a few tiny straight stitches in the white area of the neck.

6 Use 1 strand of 413 to long and short stitch between the stitching from Step 5.

7 Continue filling in the rest of the chest and neck fur. Start with 1 strand of 453 and make long and short stitches to fill the rest of the white patch. Use 1 strand of 310 to make tiny straight stitches randomly across the upper chest to give the appearance of speckles in the fur.

Face

EARS

1 Color the inside of each ear with the Tombow marker.

2 Use 1 strand of DMC BLANC to make angled straight stitches inside the left ear, around the edges. Stitch along the bottom edge, looping the thread down around the ear and into the hoop background. Make slanted straight stitches using 1 strand of 646 along the inside top of the ear. Repeat stitching with 1 strand of 648 on the inside left and bottom of the ear. Make tiny straight stitches using 1 strand of 310.

3 Use 1 strand of 310 to make straight stitches across the right that slant downwards inside the right ear. With the same thread, create 2 small spots using tiny straight stitching. Make straight stitches with 1 strand of 647 at the top and bottom of the ear. Use 1 strand of DMC BLANC to make slanted straight stitches in the upper and lower right areas of the inner ear.

4 On the outside of the ears, use a Frixion pen to mark areas that will be stitched in black (refer to the template as necessary).

5 Start with the left ear. Straight stitch over the markings with 1 strand of 310. Stem stitch around the left and top sides of the ear. Use 1 strand of 646 to straight stitch around the black speckles. Long and short stitch with 1 strand of DMC BLANC to fill in the remaining white area. Follow the shape of the black edge with 1 strand of DMC BLANC and then 1 strand of 647. At the top of the ear, wrap longer stitches over the edge of the ear into the background. Fill the remaining area with long and short stitches of 1 strand of 310.

6 On the right ear, straight stitch over the markings with 1 strand of 310. Stem stitch on the right side. Blend in long and short stitches on the right side with 1 strand of 646. Use long and short stitches in 1 strand of DMC BLANC to fill the rest of the white space. Follow the shape of the black edge with straight stitches in 1 strand of DMC BLANC and then 1 strand of 647. At the top of the ear, wrap longer stitches over the edge of the ear into the background. Fill the remaining area with long and short stitches of 1 strand of 310. Use an iron to remove all pen marks.

HEAD

TIP: At this point, using a pair of pliers will help you pull the needle through the many layers of embroidery and felt.

1 Straight stitch the gray patch between the eyes with 1 strand of 310 and 1 strand of 648. Make stitches longer around the eyes and left eyebrow and smaller in the middle. Then, fill in long and short stitches with 1 strand of 413. Add vertical straight stitches with 1 strand of DMC BLANC around the left eyebrow.

2 Use 1 strand of 647 to straight stitch the forehead and area to the left of the eyes. Add straight stitches to the forehead with 1 strand of 413. Satin stitch around the right eyebrow, and straight stitch to the lower left of the eye patch. Switch to 1 strand of 310 and make tiny seed stitches on the right side of the right eye patch, angling stitches up towards the eyes.

3 Make varying lengths of straight stitches using 1 strand of 01 to fill in spots on the left and top of the face. Angle stitches towards the eyes. Make several slanted straight stitches on the right side of the right eye patch.

EYES

1 Use 2 strands of 310 to satin stitch circles in the center of the eyes. With the same thread, back stitch around the eyes.

2 Make 1 straight stitch in the corner of each eye with 1 strand of DMC BLANC. Make two straight stitches in the bottom outside corners of both eyes. Make 2 satin stitches on the top of the left eye. Switch to 1 strand of 169. Make 1 French knot in the pupil of the left eye. Make 2 French knots in the right eye, wrapping the needle 3 times. Add a third French knot to the right eye with 1 strand of DMC BLANC.

3 Make an angled straight stitch on the outside corner of each eye with 2 strands of DMC BLANC. Follow that stitch to create eyebrows, curving the stitches away from the eyes and towards the ears. Do not pull the needle too tightly so the stitches remain curved. Slide the needle under the stitches and gently pull upward to make them more puffy and three dimensional.

4 Straight stitch around the rest of the left eye with 1 strand of DMC BLANC. Make seed stitches below the eye, angling them toward the bridge of the nose.

5 Fill out the rest of the right eyebrow with straight stitches using 1 strand of DMC BLANC. To the right of and below the right eye, use long and short stitching with the same thread, angling the stitches towards the eye. Switch to 1 strand of 310, and make small seed stitches.

6 Add more definition to the eye area by blending small straight stitches into both eyebrows and below both eyes using 1 strand of 413 and 04.

BRIDGE OF NOSE

1 Use 1 strand of 648 to make seed stitches across the bridge of the nose on the left side. With the same thread, make several straight stitches clustered upward over the top of the small oval shape on the bridge (E24).

2 Blend in more seed stitches with 1 strand of DMC BLANC. Add more straight stitches to the small oval.

3 Seed stitch with 1 strand of 646 in the middle of the bridge and the left side. On the right side of the bridge, use 1 strand of 310 and then 413 to seed stitch. Layer in straight stitches with 1 strand of DMC BLANC on the right side and along the perimeter of the small oval (E24).

MUZZLE

1 Use 1 strand of 310 to make vertical straight stitches below the nose and on the mouth. Create a single long vertical straight stitch in the middle of the nose.

2 With 1 strand of 413, make long and short stitches between the stitches from Step 1.

3 Use 1 strand of 01 to make straight stitches radiating out around the nose. Make tiny straight stitches on the lip line. Add several larger straight stitches as short whiskers below the nose.

4 With 2 strands of DMC BLANC, make long and short stitches around the nose. Slide the needle underneath the stitches and gently pull to make the stitches more three dimensional. Straight stitch the bottom of the mouth, wrapping the thread all the way around and pulling taut to make that area recede slightly.

NOSE

1 Create a highlight in the left nostril by backstitching inside the circle using 1 strand of 647. Use 1 strand of 413 to do the same in the right nostril.

2 Rub a white water soluble pencil onto the top of the nose and under each nostril to make highlights.

WHISKERS

1 Cut 13 single strands of DMC BLANC, each about 6″ in length. Lay them onto a piece of wax paper and lightly coat 3″of each strand with Stiffy Fabric Stiffener using a paintbrush. Peel up each thread and lay it straight on an unused section of wax paper to dry.

2 Thread the needle with the side of the thread that is not coated with fabric stiffener. Push the needle down into the front of the portrait, around the mouth. Pull the needle gently until it starts to drag due to the glue. Leave about an inch of stiffened thread on the outside of the portrait. Bring the needle back up along the base of the whisker. Make a tiny straight stitch over the whisker and push the needle back down to secure it. Knot the excess thread on the back of the hoop. Trim the whisker to the desired length. Manipulate the whisker's shape and position with your fingers. Repeat for all 13 whiskers.

FRAME/DISPLAY

Use the 6 ¼" Blue Spruce felt circle and DMC 502 to back the hoop as desired (see Hoop Backing, page 38). Place the hoop inside the Modern Hoopla frame, and secure with cardboard shims. Your portrait is ready to hang and admire!

Milly Cat Portrait

FINISHED PROJECT: 6″ × 6″

Cats have an uncanny air of aloofness that can be both mesmerizing and exasperating when attempting portraiture. Milly, my in-laws' cat, is the epitome of both intensity and indifference, making her the perfect feline model. This project highlights the importance of intricately layering felt, and how it can be used to create three dimensional facial features, such as eye hollows and a protruding mouth. Combining this sculptural technique with thread painting brings Milly to life and captures her ever elusive glare.

MATERIALS

- 4" embroidery hoop
- Sizes 8, 6, and 4 embroidery needles
- Fiskars Micro-Tip Scissors
- Milly Cat Templates (page 15)
- Quilter's Freezer Paper Sheets
- Frixion Heat Erasable Pen
- Iron
- Art Markers: Tombow ABT N52, ABT N60, Pro PN69, Pro PN79 and Pro P992
- White water soluble pencil
- E6000 Glue
- Hot glue and glue gun
- Cardstock
- Paintbrush
- Wax paper
- Pliers (optional)
- Modern Hoopla Square Frame (natural finish)

THREAD AND FELT

- 1 sheet 9″ × 12″ Wasabi Bellwether felt
- 1 sheet 9″ × 12″ Morel Bellwether felt
- 1 sheet 9″ × 12″ White Truffle felt
- 1 sheet 9″ × 12″ Lunar Bellwether
- 1 sheet 9″ × 12″ Meringue felt
- 1 sheet 9″ × 12″ Shortbread felt
- 1 sheet 9″ × 12″ Linen felt
- 1 sheet 9″ × 12″ Castle felt
- 1 sheet 9″ × 12″ Black felt
- 1 sheet 9″ × 12″ Grapefruit felt
- 1 sheet 9″ × 12″ Agave Bellwether felt

DMC six-stranded cotton embroidery floss (1 skein of each)

B5200, BLANC, 03, 07, 08, 168, 169, 310, 368, 434, 451, 453, 612, 613, 646, 677, 738, 762, 840, 3022, 3364, 3371, 3770, 3778, 3782, 3787, 3790, 3861, 3866

Milly
Milly

Cut felt pieces for Milly

Layered felt pieces for Milly

CUT LIST

Transfer the Milly Cat Templates to the felt using freezer paper and cut them out as directed below (see Transferring Templates, page 19). I do not recommend using a Frixion pen for transferring templates with this pattern because the pieces are so small and intricate. Make sure all pieces are labeled.

Background and Backing

Cut 1 circle 5¼″ diameter from Wasabi felt (bark background).

Cut 1 circle 4¼″ diameter from cardstock (hoop backing).

Cat

Cut 1 Template M1, M3, M5, M6, M7 and M14 from Morel Bellwether felt.

Cut 1 Template M2 from White Truffle felt.

Cut 1 Template M4 Lunar Bellwether felt.

Cut 1 Template M8 and M9 from Meringue felt.

Cut 1 Template M10, M11, M26 and M27 from Shortbread felt.

Cut 1 Template M12 and M15 from Linen felt.

Cut 1 Template M13 and M16 from Castle felt.

Cut 1 Template M17, M19 and M20 from Black felt.

Cut 2 Templates M25 from Black felt.

Cut 1 Template M18 from Grapefruit felt.

Cut 1 Template M21 and M22 from Wasabi Bellwether felt.

Cut 1 Template M23 and M24 from Agave Bellwether felt.

Text Ribbon

Cut 1 Template M28 from Linen felt.

Cut 1 Template M29 from Morel Bellwether felt.

PREPARE THE HOOP

Place and tighten the 5¼″ Wasabi felt circle into the 4″ embroidery hoop.

FELT APPLIQUÉ

During the felt appliqué process, use 1 strand of embroidery floss and a size 8 needle. Unless otherwise stated, attach each piece with a running stitch around the perimeter, leaving a ¹⁄₁₆″ seam allowance.

1 Place M1 in the middle of the hoop, and stitch down with 08.

2 Layer M2 over M1, matching edges, and attach with 613.

3 Put M3 over M2, matching edges, and stitch with 08.

4 Position M4 over M3, centering it and matching ears, and attach with 168.

5 Layer M5 over M4, matching edges, and stitch down with 08.

6 Position M6 on the right edge of the left ear and M7 on the left edge of the right ear. Use a blanket appliqué stitch and 1 strand of 08 to attach to M5. Space stitches about ⅛″ apart.

7 Place M8 on the left edge of the left ear and M9 on the right edge of the right ear. Running stitch up the center (the thinnest area) and then around the perimeter of the base with 3770.

8 Position M10 in the left eye hollow of M3 and M11 in the right hollow. Stitch with 738.

9 Layer M12 over the bottom of M5 and attach with 3866.

10 Place M13 over the upper part of M12 and part of M5. Stitch with 3782.

11 Position M14 just above M13, and affix with 08.

12 Layer M15 at the bottom of M13 so it borders M12. Stitch with 3866.

13 Place M16, triangular end down, against the border of M15. Attach with 3782.

14 Position M17 at the bottom of M16, up against M15. Affix with 310.

15 Layer M18 in the middle of M17. Make 1 straight stitch in each of the 3 corners with 3778.

16 Place M19 in the right corner of M10, up against M5. Place M20 in the left corner of M11, up against M5. Stitch M19 and M20 with 310.

17 Position M21 in the middle of M19 and M22 in the middle of M20. Attach with 3364.

18 Place M23 in the middle and along the top of M21. Place M24 in the middle and along the top of M22. Affix with 368.

19 Layer 1 M25 in the center of M23 and 1 in the middle of M24. Make 1 straight stitch with 310 in the middle of each piece.

20 Position M26 over the left eye and M27 over the right eye. Running stitch along the middle with 738.

EMBROIDERY

Varying the length, direction, and type of embroidery stitches makes the features of this cat really come to life. Use needles with larger eyes when using more than 3 strands of thread or if you are stitching through more than 7 layers of felt. A size 6 needle will work for most of the steps, but you may want to switch to size 4 needle for the final embroidery steps. Refer to the stitch library (page 26) for step-by-step instructions for each embroidery stitch used in this project.

Ears

1 Use 1 strand of 3866 to fill the inside of the ears with diagonal, overlapping straight and stem stitches.

2 Gently shade the lower areas of the ears with Tombow PN79 and Tombow P992 markers. Across from the stitching in Step 1, use PN79, PN52 and N52 markers to add definition and shading.

3 Using 1 strand of 612, create short straight stitches along the brown edges of the ears. Stitch between the Step 1 stitches with long and short stitch.

4 Stem stitch along the outside of the ears and around the tips with 2 strands of 738.

5 At the base of each ear, make straight stitches of various lengths using 1 strand of 738.

Nose and Mouth

1 Create small seed stitches on the left and right sides of the muzzle with 1 strand of 310.

2 Use 1 strand of 310 to make a single straight stitch in the middle of the nose. Switch to 1 strand of 451, and sprinkle several small straight stitches on each side of the muzzle. Use 1 strand of 169 to make diagonal long and short stitches on the right side of M12. Using 1 strand of 03 and 453, add long and short stitches around the muzzle and mouth to define the mouth crease.

3 Working on either side of the nostrils, use 1 strand of 738 to make slanted straight stitches.

4 Long and short stitch with 1 strand 762 on the top of the mouth. Use 1 strand of DMC B5200 to fill in more long and short stitches.

5 Use 1 strand 3790 to seed stitch toward the bridge of the nose. Make an upside down *U*-shape above the nose using vertical straight stitches.

6 Use a white water soluble pencil to color a small highlighted spot above the nose.

7 Add a single straight stitch at the mouth opening using 1 strand of 3371. Add slanted seed stitches away from the nose. Make longer seed stitches in the lower part of the eye hollows slanted up toward the eyes.

8 Using a single strand of 3371, add tiny vertical seed stitches up the bridge of the nose. Straight stitch down from the eye hollow stitches. Fill in the muzzle and nose with seed stitches.

9 Use 1 strand of 3787 to fill the piece between the eyes with vertical seed stitches.

10 Continue adding more seed stitches to the same area with 1 strand of 677. Fill the right half with more and longer stitches.

Cheeks

1 Long and short stitch with 1 strand 3782, to stitch from the base of the cat's face over the edge and onto the background felt. Slant the stitches toward the nose. Blend in long and short stitches with 1 strand of 07 and 08 to fill the next section up.

2 On the right side of the cheek, long and short stitch with 1 strand of 3866, slanting the stitches. Use 1 strand of 3022 to make small seed stitches between the long and short stitches. Create 2 small spots in the middle of the cheek with slanted seed stitches: the bottom spot with 1 strand of 612 and the top spot with 1 strand of 3787. Extend the long and short stitches of 3866 up the cheek. Layer in 1 strand of 613 long and short stitches.

3 On the left cheek, layer in a gradient of long and short stitches, starting at the edge closest to the mouth. Using 1 strand of each color, layer in 07, 08, 3782, and 840. Allow some of the felt to show through. Finally, add small satin stitches with 1 strand of 3371 just above the 08 stitches.

Under Eyes

1 Use 1 strand of 738 to long and short stitch just below the eyes. Slant the stitches towards the eyes.

2 Make small seed stitches slanted towards the bridge of the nose in the corners of the Step 1 stitching with 1 strand of 434. Above that, make 2 small, slanted seed stitches with 1 strand of 840 for each eye.

3 Below the eyes, use 1 strand of 738 to create seed stitches slanted towards the bridge of the nose. Layer in more seed stitches with 1 strand 3371. On the left cheek, make long and short stitches angled towards the bridge of the nose with 1 strand of 738.

4 On the right cheek, make long and short stitches with 1 strand of 3866 and 3782 to stitch up to the beginning of the forehead.

5 To the right of the eyebrow, make several stacked horizontal straight stitches with 1 strand of 3371. Switch to 1 strand of 3787 and make straight stitches that slant towards the eyes along the rest of the edge.

6 Working on the left cheek, use 1 strand of 08 to make horizontal seed stitches in the open areas. Repeat Step 5 for the left eye, working along the edge of the other eyebrow.

Top of the Head

1 Use a Frixion pen to mark dark striped areas on the top of the head (refer to template M5 as necessary).

2 Stitch over the marks with long and short stitches using 1 strand of 3371. Use an iron to remove pen marks.

3 Use 1 strand of 3782 to make straight stitches between the two open stripes in the middle of the forehead. Use 1 strand of 738 to create seed stitches in between the remaining stripes.

4 Working on the left side of the head below the ear, use 1 strand of 738 to make long and short stitches in a slightly wavy stripe. Slant the stitches toward the ear. Make tiny seed stitches in between the stripes.

5 Moving to the right side of the head, below the ear, use 1 strand of 3782 to make long and short stitches in a stripe. Slant the stitches towards the ear. Create several long and short stitches above the stripe. Add in straight stitches at the right with 1 strand of 738, then fill in seed stitches.

6 Seed stitch across the head using 1 strand of 3371. Leave some of the felt showing through.

7 On the outer, bottom edges of both sides of the head, use 1 strand of 612 to make straight stitches that slant stitches toward the eyes.

Eyes

1 Just below the inner corners of both eyes, make 4–5 tiny straight stitches with 1 strand of 3861. Make seed stitches that follow the shape of the brows using 1 strand of 738. At the ends of the eyebrows, just above each eye, use 1 strand of 3770 to integrate a dozen straight stitches.

2 On the left eye, use 2 strands of 310 to outline the top with long back stitches. Repeat on the right eye with only 1 strand of 310. Use the same thread to outline the pupils. Bring the needle up at the base of the left pupil and then back down at the top of the pupil, holding the thread to the side before pulling tight, to ensure it curves around the shape. Repeat for the other side of the left pupil and then on the right pupil.

3 Use 1 strand of 3787 to stem stitch around the black outlines at the bottom of each eye. Straight stitch the left corner of the right eye and along the black line's curve with 1 strand of 03. Use 1 strand of 646 to straight stitch the right corner of the left eye, following the curve.

4 Lightly shade the irises of both eyes with a Tombow ABT N60 art marker. Shade only the left sides and top of the irises.

5 Make one French knot in each eye near the tops of the pupils using 1 strand of DMC BLANC. Use 1 strand of 01 and wrap the thread around the needle three times to add 1 French knot slightly down and to the right of each previous knot.

6 Use 1 strand of 762 to make 3 satin stitches along the edge of the right iris. Make one straight stitch in the right corner of the left iris.

Eyebrow Whiskers

Make multiple straight stitches and 2 fly stitches to create whiskers above the eyebrows with 1 strand of DMC BLANC. For the 2 fly stitches, use 2 anchor stitches to make the thread more curved.

FRAME

Flip the hoop over. Trim the back of the Wasabi circle, as flush to the hoop as possible. Place the hoop inside a 4″ Modern Hoopla square frame with natural stain. Use shims to secure the hoop.

TEXT BANNER

1 Make an accordion fold along the dotted lines of M28. Iron along the folds to create creases.

2 Use a Frixion pen to handwrite "Milly" across M28 (see template). Add horizontal serifs to the ends of the letters.

3 Use 2 strands of 310 to straight stitch the letters, excluding the serifs. Add a French knot for the top of the "i".

4 Use 1 strand of 310 to make small straight stitches for the serifs. Use an iron to remove pen marks.

5 Make long straight stitches between the top and bottom serifs on the right side of each letter.

6 Hot glue the ends of M28 to M29. Leave the middle of M28 unglued so it pops away from M29.

7 Spread a thin layer of E6000 around the bottom ⅔ of M29, along the perimeter. Attach to the top of the frame.

WHISKERS

1 Cut 15 single strands of DMC BLANC, each about 7″ in length. Lay them onto a piece of wax paper and lightly coat 3–4″of each strand with Stiffy Fabric Stiffener using a paintbrush. Peel up each thread, and lay it straight on an unused section of wax paper to dry.

2 Thread the needle with the side of the thread that is not coated with fabric stiffener. Push the needle down into the front of the portrait, around the mouth. Pull the needle gently until it starts to drag due to the glue. Leave several inches of stiffened thread on the outside of the portrait. Bring the needle back up along the base of the whisker. Make a tiny straight stitch over the whisker and push the needle back down to secure it. Knot the excess thread on the back of the hoop.

3 Trim the whisker to the desired length. Manipulate the whisker's shape and position with your fingers. Repeat for all 15 whiskers.

BACK THE HOOP

Because the hoop is already set in a frame, it is easier to glue the backing rather than attempt to stitch it. Use the 4 ¼" cardstock circle to back the hoop (see Hoop Backing, page 38).

Turkey Tail Mushrooms

FINISHED PROJECT: 5¼″ × 4½″ × 2½″

Mushrooms are fascinating! Out of the darkest, dreariest spots of decay, come the most beautifully intricate shapes and patterns. I recently found a turkey tail cluster while hiking around the woods outside my house, and was so taken by its rings of color and levitating fan formations. Much like the gravity-defying feats of the Turkey Tail Mushroom, this project elevates felt appliqué to a sculptural level.

MATERIALS

4" embroidery hoop
Size 8 embroidery needle
Kai N5000 Scissors
Turkey Tail Templates (page 15)
Quilter's Freezer Paper Sheets or Frixion Pen
Iron
Wash-away stabilizer transfer paper
E6000 Glue
Tombow ABT Pro Art Marker: PN49 (optional)
Modern Hoopla Hoop Stand (walnut finish)

DMC six-stranded cotton embroidery floss (1 skein of each)

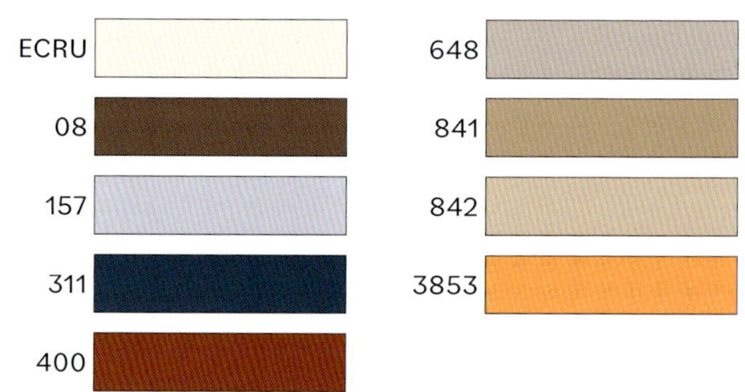

THREAD AND FELT

1 sheet 9″ × 12″ Morel Bellwether felt
1 sheet 9″ × 12″ Oyster Bellwether felt
1 sheet 9″ × 12″ Sky felt
1 sheet 9″ × 12″ Terrazzo Bellwether felt
1 sheet 9″ × 12″ Pool felt
1 sheet 9″ × 12″ Umber Bellwether felt

Cut felt pieces for mushrooms

CUT LIST

Transfer the Turkey Tail Templates to the felt using freezer paper or a Frixion pen, and cut them out as directed below (see Transferring Templates, page 19). Make sure to label each piece.

Background and Backing

Cut 1 circle 5¼″ diameter from Morel felt (bark background).

Cut 1 circle 4¼″ diameter from Morel felt (hoop backing).

Large Mushroom

Cut 2 Templates L1 from Oyster felt.

Cut 1 Template L2 from Sky felt.

Cut 1 Template L3 and L6 from Terrazzo felt.

Cut 1 Template L4 from Pool felt.

Cut 1 Template L5 from Umber felt.

Medium and Small Mushrooms

Cut 2 Templates M1 and S1 from Oyster felt.

Cut 1 Template M4 and S4 from Oyster felt.

Cut 1 Template M2 and S2 from Sky felt.

Cut 1 Template M3 and S3 from Pool felt.

Cut 1 Template M5 and S5 from Umber felt.

Cut 1 Template M6 and S6 from Terrazzo felt.

PREPARE THE BACKGROUND

Refer to the stitch library (page 26) for step-by-step instructions for each embroidery stitch used in this project.

1 Print the bark pattern onto the wash-away paper. Attach it to the 5¼″ Morel felt circle.

2 Use 3 strands of 08 to stem stitch the bark lines. Do not stitch the circle outlines.

3 Wash away the paper, and allow the felt to dry.

4 Optional: Color the embroidery hoop by brushing it with the Tombow PN49 so that it better matches the color palette of the felt.

5 Tighten the bark felt circle in the hoop. This project will be displayed in the hoop stand with the clasp facing down, so position the bark direction accordingly.

FELT APPLIQUÉ

For this section, split stitch with 4 strands of embroidery floss, and stem stitch with 3 strands.

Small and Medium Mushrooms

1 Set one S1 piece aside. Layer S2 over the other S1, centering and lining up the flat edges. Split stitch along the curved outer edge of S2 with 648. Do not stitch along the straight edge of the mushroom.

2 Stem stitch along the split stitch you just made with DMC ECRU.

3 Layer S3 over S2. Split stitch along the outer edge of S3 with 311.

4 Layer S4 over S3. Split stitch along the outer edge of S4 with 157.

5 Layer S5 over S4. Split stitch along the outer edge of S5 with 3853.

6. Layer S6 over S5. Split stitch along the outer edge of S6 with 841.

Completed small and medium mushrooms

7 Repeat Steps 1–6 to create the Medium Mushroom using pieces M1-M6 and the same thread colors.

Large Mushroom

1 Set one L1 piece aside. Layer L2 over the other L1, centering and lining up the flat edges. Split stitch along the curved outer edge of L2 with 400. Do not stitch along the straight edge of the mushroom.

2 Stem stitch along the split stitch you just made with DMC ECRU.

3 Layer L3 over L2. Split stitch along the outer edge of L3 with 311.

4 Layer L4 over L3. Split stitch along the outer edge of L4 with 157.

5 Layer L5 over L4. Split stitch along the outer edge of L5 with 3853.

6 Stem stitch along the split stitch you just made with 648.

7 Layer L6 over L5. Split stitch along the outer edge of L6 with 841.

Embroidered Mushroom Tops

SPORES

With 2 strands of 842, make French knots over the second set of S1, M1 and L1 pieces. Be sporadic (pun very much intended) with the number of knots and the knot placement for a more natural look.

FINISH MUSHROOMS

1 Place the small, medium, and large felt mushrooms over the spore covered S1, M1 and L1 pieces respectively (small mushroom with S1), keeping the French knots facing down and away from the mushroom tops. Blanket stitch them together with 1 strand of 842 along the outer edge. Do not stitch along the straight edge of the mushrooms.

2 Use your fingers to twist the edges of the mushroom shelves to make them slightly curved.

ATTACH MUSHROOMS TO BARK BACKGROUND

Attach mushrooms with the spore side facing down toward the clasp.

Placement of Large Mushroom

1 Position the large mushroom shelf in the center right side of the hoop. Blanket stitch appliqué the spore bottom edge of the large mushroom shelf to the bark hoop with 2 strands of 842. The top of the mushroom should still pull away from the hoop.

2 Glue the top of the large mushroom shelf to the felt using E6000 glue. Please note that cure time is up to 24 hrs, so it is important to press firmly and then lie the piece flat to ensure it has cured properly.

3 Repeat Steps 1–2 for the small and medium mushroom shelves. Position the medium mushroom shelf below and to the left of the large mushroom. Position the small mushroom shelf above and to the left of the large mushroom.

DISPLAY

Use the 4¼″ Morel felt circle and DMC 08 to back the hoop (see Hoop Backing, page 38). Place the finished piece clasp-side down into the Modern Hoopla hoop stand. Because this project is top heavy, you may need to use a folded cardboard shim inside of the hoop stand for added support.

Oyster Mushrooms

FINISHED PROJECT SIZE: 10¼″ x 7¼″

When I was young, I would spend hours outside building fairy houses and creating little scenes in our backyard. Some of my favorite treasures were mushrooms, moss, and lichen. This piece takes me right back to those days of imagining fairies gathering at dusk for a banquet under mushroom tops. In this project, you will emulate the different textures and depths of a fairyscape by using felt appliqué, padded stumpwork, and a variety of stitches.

MATERIALS

5" x 8" oval embroidery hoop
Size 7 and 3 embroidery needles
Kai N5000 Scissors
Oyster Mushroom Templates (page 15)
Quilter's Freezer Paper Sheets
Frixion Heat Erasable Pen
Iron
Poly-Fil
Benzie Design Stuffing Tool
Hot glue gun and glue
Modern Hoopla Oval Frame (walnut finish)

THREAD AND FELT

1 sheet 12″ x 18″ Turquoise felt
1 sheet 9″ x 12″ Oyster Bellwether felt
1 sheet 9″ x 12″ Cashmere Bellwether felt
1 sheet 9″ x 12″ Nori Bellwether felt
1 sheet 9″ x 12″ Zucchini felt
1 sheet 9″ x 12″ Laurel Bellwether felt
1 sheet 9″ x 12″ Mint felt

DMC six-stranded cotton embroidery floss (1 skein of each)

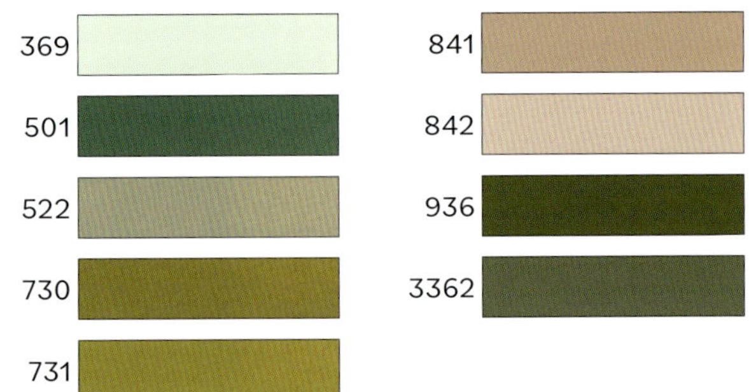

Cut felt pieces for mushrooms

Cut felt pieces for moss and lichen

CUT LIST

Transfer the Oyster Mushroom Templates to the felt using freezer paper or Frixion pen and cut them out as directed below (see Transferring Templates, page 19). I recommend using freezer paper for all pieces except for the gills. Because there are so many gill pieces, using a Frixion pen is more efficient.

Background & Backing

Cut 1 oval 6½″ × 9¾″ from Turquoise felt (background).

Cut 1 oval 5″ × 8¼″ from Turquoise felt (hoop backing).

Oyster Mushrooms

Cut 2 Templates O1 from Oyster Bellwether felt.

Cut 1 Template O2 from Oyster Bellwether felt.

Cut 10 Templates O5 from Oyster Bellwether felt.

Cut 7 Templates O6 from Oyster Bellwether felt.

Cut 2 Templates O3 from Cashmere Bellwether felt.

Cut 1 Template O4 from Cashmere Bellwether felt.

Moss

Cut 1 Template M1, M4 and M5 from Nori Bellwether felt.

Cut 1 Template M2 and M3 from Zucchini felt.

Lichen

Cut 1 Template L1, L2, L3, L4, L6, L7, and L9 from Laurel Bellwether felt.

Cut 1 Template L2, L3, L5, L6, L8 and L10 from Mint felt.

PREPARE THE HOOP

Place and tighten the 6½″ × 9¾″ Turquoise oval into the embroidery hoop.

OYSTER MUSHROOMS

Unless otherwise stated, use a size 7 needle for this project. Refer to the stitch library (page 26) for step-by-step instructions for each embroidery stitch used in this project.

Attach Gills to Oyster Mushrooms

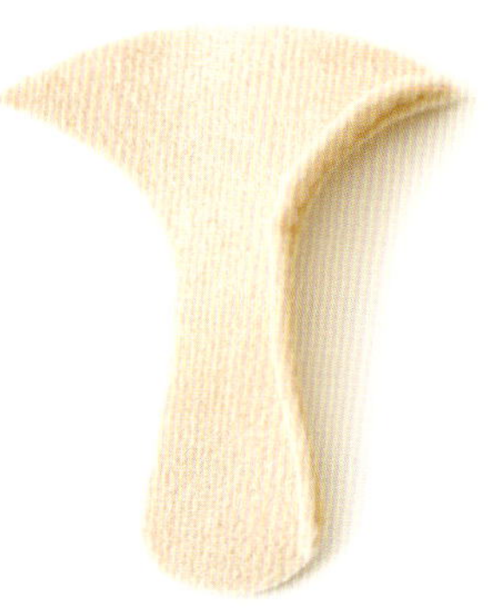

1 Layer 1 gill (O5) over 1 Template O1 piece, ⅛″ from the edge, and with the angled tip facing down. Following the curve, whip stitch with 1 strand of 842.

2 Iron the gill in the opposite direction so that it sticks straight up.

3 Place another gill on the unit about ⅛″ away from the first gill. Attach with a whip stitch with 1 strand of 842. This gill will curve less, and the top will end about ½″ away from the top of the previous gill. Iron so that it stands upright.

4 Repeat Step 3 for the remaining 3 gills, placing the third gill in the middle of the mushroom base, and then fanning the last 2 gills out in the opposite direction.

5 Repeat Steps 1–4 for the other O1 mushroom.

6 Repeat Steps 1–4 for the O2 mushroom using O6 gills. In this case, the middle gill is the fourth one, with 3 gills on each side.

Attach Mushrooms to the Hoop

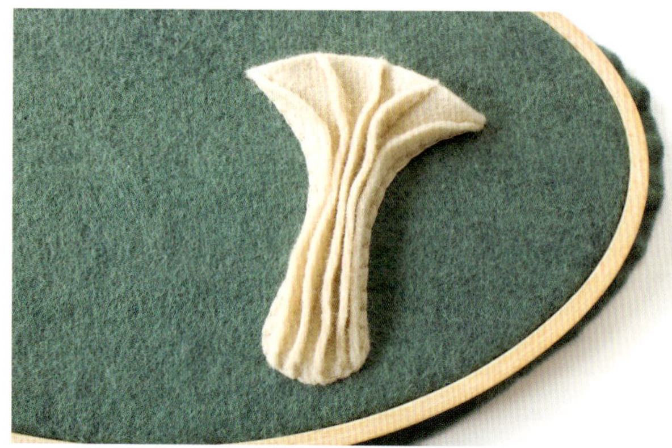

1 Position the prepped hoop horizontally. Place 1 small mushroom (O1) to the right of the middle of the hoop, about ¾″ from the hoop's bottom edge. Start at one corner of the mushroom and blanket stitch appliqué it to the hoop using 1 strand of 842. Stitch around to the other corner of the top, leaving the rounded top edge open.

2 Use filling and the stuffing tool to pad the base of the mushroom. Leave a generous amount in the top.

3 Place O3 over the top of the small mushroom. Use 2 strands of 841 to blanket stitch along the outer edge of the mushroom. Then, using the same thread, blanket appliqué the flat edge of O3 to the background felt.

4 Repeat Steps 1–3 for the other two mushrooms, using O4 for the larger mushroom. Place the largest mushroom in the middle of the hoop, and the other small mushroom to the left at an angle.

5 Use a size 3 needle and 6 strands of 841 to loop through the blanket stitched edges of each mushroom top, adding dimension.

EMBELLISHING THE BACKGROUND

Felt Appliqué Moss

1 Place M3 at the bottom right of the right mushroom. Blanket appliqué it to the hoop with 1 strand of 730. Before closing, pad with filling using the stuffing tool.

2 Repeat Step 1 for M2, placing it at the bottom left of the left mushroom.

3 Repeat Step 1 for M1, centering it to overlap the bottom of all three mushrooms. Use 1 strand of 936.

4 Place M5 over M2, centering it and lining up the bottom edges. Blanket appliqué M5 with 1 strand of 936. Before closing, stuff with filling.

5 Place M4 over M3, centering it and lining up the bottom edges. Repeat Step 4 to attach.

Embroidered Moss

1 Make French knots over M2 using 2 strands of 730.

2 Use 1 strand 936 and create varying sizes of cross stitches over M5.

3 Repeat Step 1 on the right side.

4 Use 3 strands of 3362 to seed stitch across the center patch.

5 Create French knots among the seed stitches in Step 4 with 1 strand of 731.

6 Use 1 strand 3362 to seed stitch between the stitches in Steps 4 and 5. Pull the seed stitches tight to pucker the felt and create a dimpled effect.

Lichen

1 Layer first large lichen cluster from bottom to top as follows: L1, L2, L3 (Laurel) and L3 (Mint). Stagger the L3 pieces so part of the Laurel layer sticks out around the side of the Mint layer. Use 1 strand of 369 to create a feather stitch along the top piece.

2 Layer the second large lichen cluster from bottom to top as follows: L4, L5, L6 (Laurel) and L6 (Mint). Repeat Step 1 to assemble.

3 Layer L8 over L7. Layer L10 over L9. Use 1 strand of 369 to create a feather stitch along L8 and L10.

4 Place the L9/L10 lichen cluster between the base of the left mushroom and moss (M2). Use 1 strand 522, and create small straight stitches to anchor L10 to the hoop.

5 Place the L7/L8 lichen cluster between the base of the right mushroom and moss (M3). Use 1 strand of 522, and create small straight stitches to anchor L8 to the hoop.

FRAME AND FINISH

1 Use the 5″ × 8 ¼″ Turquoise felt oval and DMC 501 to back the hoop (see Hoop Backing, page 38). Place hoop in Modern Hoopla oval frame with walnut finish. Use cardboard shims to secure.

2 Place lichen cluster L1-L3 to the left of the left moss cluster. Hot glue to the frame and slightly inside the hoop.

3 Place lichen cluster L4-L6 to the right of the right moss cluster. Hot glue to the frame and slightly inside the hoop.

African Flower Beetle with Leaves

FINISHED PROJECT: 7¾″ x 7½″

Years ago, I visited a museum that had an entire room devoted to insects. There were floor to ceiling walls covered in glass cases full of precisely tacked bugs. I was especially drawn to the beetles, which looked almost otherworldly with their hard shells, prickly legs, and intricate wings. Much like those insects in the museum, this project gives the feeling of a real beetle on display. To achieve a more lifelike effect, this piece combines felt appliqué with padded stumpwork. Embroidery and a realistic leaf border add to the three dimensionality of the project.

MATERIALS

- 6" embroidery hoop
- Sizes 10, 7, and 5 embroidery needles
- Fiskars Micro-Tip Scissors
- African Flower Beetle with Leaves Templates (page 15)
- Quilter's Freezer Paper sheets
- Frixion Heat Erasable Pen
- Iron
- Wash-away stabilizer transfer paper
- Poly-Fil
- Benzie Design Stuffing Tool
- Hot glue gun and glue

THREAD AND FELT

- 1 sheet 12″ x 18″ Custard Bellwether felt
- 1 sheet 9″ x 12″ Sherwood Bellwether felt
- 1 sheet 9″ x 12″ Emerald felt
- 1 sheet 9″ x 12″ Saffron Bellwether felt
- 1 sheet 9″ x 12″ Chicory Bellwether felt
- 1 sheet 9″ x 12″ Ochre felt
- 1 sheet 9″ x 12″ Zucchini felt
- 1 sheet 9″ x 12″ Nori Bellwether felt

DMC six-stranded cotton embroidery floss (1 skein of each)

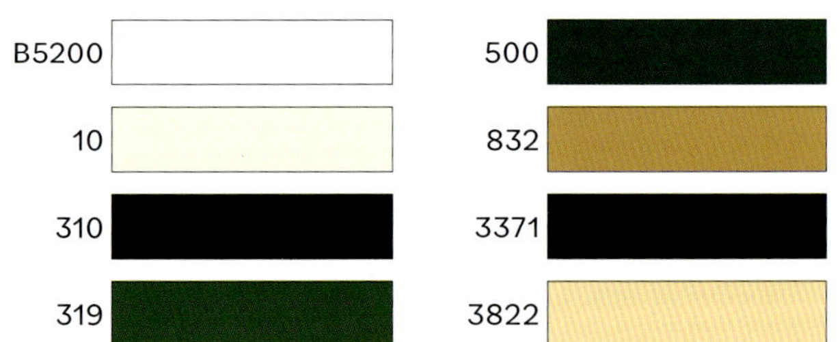

Cut felt pieces for beetle

Cut felt pieces for leaves

CUT LIST

Transfer the African Flower Beetle Templates to the felt using freezer paper and cut them out as directed below (see Transferring Templates, page 19). I do not recommend using a Frixion pen for this project due to the dark colored felt used. Do not cut along dotted and solid lines within templates, as these are placement and stitch guidelines. Make sure each piece is labeled.

Background & Backing

Cut 1 circle 7″ diameter from Custard Bellwether felt (background).

Cut 1 circle 6¼″ diameter from Custard Bellwether felt (hoop backing).

Beetle

Cut 1 Template B1, B2 and B11 from Sherwood Bellwether felt.

Cut 1 Template B3, B4, B5, B6 and B12 from Emerald felt.

Cut 1 Template B7 and B8 from Saffron Bellwether felt.

Cut 1 Template B9, B10 and B13 from Chicory Bellwether felt.

Cut 1 Template B14, B15, B16, B17 and B18 from Ochre felt.

Leaves

Cut 6–7 Templates L1 from Zucchini felt.

Cut 6–7 Templates L1 from Nori Bellwether felt.

PREPARE THE HOOP

Place and tighten the 7″ Custard Bellwether felt circle into the hoop.

AFRICAN FLOWER BEETLE

Use a size 7 embroidery needle unless otherwise noted. Refer to the stitch library (page 26) for step-by-step instructions for each embroidery stitch used in this project.

Lower Body

Use 500 to attach all pieces of the lower body and stitch leg details.

1 Use 1 strand to running stitch B1 to the center of the background felt. Stitch around the perimeter with a 1⁄16″ seam allowance.

2 Place B11 at the top of B1. Use 1 strand to running stitch to the background felt. Stitch around the perimeter with a 1⁄16″ seam allowance.

3 With a Frixion pen, draw ½″ straight lines coming out from the top two legs and the bottom two legs. Split stitch on the lines with 4 strands. Use an iron to remove any pen marks.

4 Use 2 strands to make 2 small straight stitches at the end of each leg.

Wings

1 Place B7 and B8 slightly over B1 on either side (see Template B1 for placement). Running stitch with 1 strand of 832.

2 Layer B9 on B7 and B10 on B8. Running stitch with 1 strand of 3371. Make a single line of stitches down the narrowest sections, and keep a seam allowance of 1⁄16″ around the perimeter of the bases.

3 Draw wing veins with a Frixion pen (refer to templates B7 and B8 as necessary). Stem stitch along the lines with 2 strands of 3371. Use an iron to remove any pen marks.

Body and Head

1 Layer B2 over the body and wings, aligning the edges. Running stitch with 1 strand of 500 around the perimeter, keeping a 1⁄16″ seam allowance.

2 Layer B12 over B11. Running stitch with 1 strand of 319 up the center and in the middle of each curve.

3 Layer B13 over B12. Make 5 running stitches with 1 strand of 3371 to secure.

4 With a size 5 embroidery needle and 2 strands of 310, make French knots on both sides of B11 to create eyes.

5 With 1 strand of DMC B5200, make a tiny straight stitch within each French knot.

6 Layer B14, B15, and B16 over B3 (see Template B3 for placement). Running stitch up the center of each with 1 strand of 3822.

7 Blanket appliqué B3 over B2 with 1 strand of 319, aligning edges. Before closing fully, stuff lightly with filling and the stuffing tool.

8 In between B14 and B16, and B16 and B15, make 3 long satin stitches with 1 strand of 3822 to create stripes.

9 Layer B4 over B3. Running stitch around the perimeter with 1 strand of 319. Keep a 1/16" seam allowance.

Outer Wings

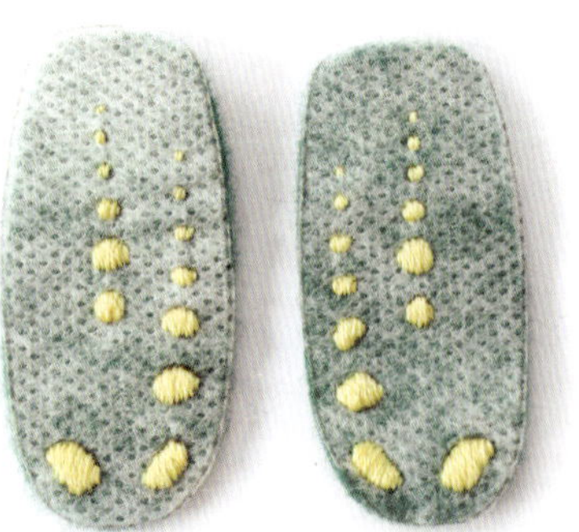

1 Print the Beetle Wing Pattern onto wash-away paper. Attach printed paper to B5 and B6 (see Transferring Templates, page 19).

2 Satin stitch the beetle wing circles using a size 10 needle and 2 strands of 3822. Wash away the paper, and let it dry.

3 Layer B17 over B5 and B18 over B6. Running stitch up the center of each with 1 strand of 3822.

4 Blanket stitch appliqué B5 and B6 over B4 with 1 strand of 319. Slightly angle B5 and B6 to match the side edges of B6, leaving a small gap between the pieces.

LEAVES

1 Fold all leaves in half, and iron to crease in the middle.

2 Hot glue the leaves around the hoop, alternating colors and overlapping them. You may choose to use as many or few leaves as you want.

BACK THE HOOP/DISPLAY

Use the 6 ¼" Custard Bellwether felt circle and DMC 10 to back the hoop (see Hoop Backing, page 38). Display this in its hoop so the leaves are not disturbed.

Io Moth with Moon Phases

FINISHED PROJECT: 8¾″ × 8¾″

Moths often have a reputation for being the uglier, drabber cousins of butterflies. But many moth species, including the bright yellow Io Moth, are just as colorful and distinctive. This night flyer is known for having large eye spots that mimic animal eyes and scare away predators. The moon phases around the frame help to tie the project together, honoring the moth's nocturnal habits and also mimicking the "eyes" on the back of its wings.

MATERIALS

6" embroidery hoop
Sizes 10, 7, 5, and 3 embroidery needles
Kai N5000 Scissors
Io Moth with Moon Phases Templates (page 15)
Quilter's Freezer Paper Sheets
Frixion Heat Erasable Pen
Iron
Wash-away stabilizer transfer paper
Poly-Fil
Benzie Design Stuffing Tool
Pliers (optional)
E6000 Glue
Modern Hoopla Circle Frame (black finish)

THREAD AND FELT

1 sheet 12″ × 18″ Fig Bellwether felt
1 sheet 9″ × 12″ Lemonade felt
1 sheet 9″ × 12″ Dandelion felt
1 sheet 9″ × 12″ Mulberry felt
1 sheet 9″ × 12″ Black felt
1 sheet 9″ × 12″ Slate Bellwether felt
1 sheet 9″ × 12″ White felt

DMC six-stranded cotton embroidery floss (1 skein of each)

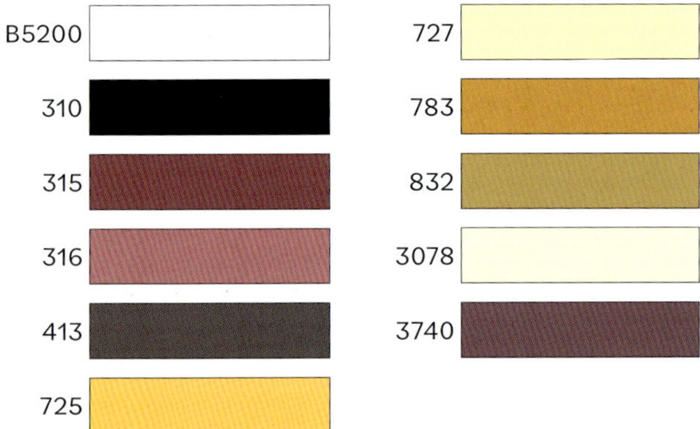

Cut felt pieces for moth

Cut felt pieces for moons

CUT LIST

Transfer the Io Moth Templates to the felt using freezer paper, and cut them out as directed below (see Transferring Templates, page 19). A heat erasable pen and soluble pencil will also work for this pattern. Do not cut along dotted and solid lines within templates, as these are placement and stitch guidelines. Make sure to label each piece.

Background & Backing

Cut 1 circle 7″ diameter from Fig Bellwether felt (background).

Cut 1 circle 6¼″ diameter from Fig Bellwether felt (hoop backing).

Moth

Cut 1 Template M1 from Lemonade felt.

Cut 1 Template M2 and M8 from Dandelion felt.

Cut 1 Template M3 and M4 from Mulberry felt.

Cut 2 Templates M5 from Black felt.

Cut 2 Templates M6 from Slate Bellwether felt.

Cut 2 Templates M7 from Lemonade felt.

Moon Phases

Cut 8 Templates M9 from Fig Bellwether felt.

Cut 7 Templates M10 from Slate Bellwether felt.

Cut 1 Template M10 from White felt.

Cut 2 Templates M11, M12 and M13 from White felt.

PREPARE THE HOOP

Place and tighten the 7″ Fig Bellwether felt circle into the 6″ embroidery hoop.

CREATING THE IO MOTH

Unless otherwise stated, use a size 7 needle for stitching. Refer to the stitch library (page 26) for step-by-step instructions for each embroidery stitch used in this project.

Felt Appliqué Lower Body

1 Place M1 in the middle of the hoop. Use 1 strand 727 to blanket stitch appliqué M1 to the felt background.

2 Draw 2 slightly curved lines, about ¾″ in length, coming out from the head with a Frixion pen. Use 2 strands of 725 to stem stitch over the lines. Draw a round feather shape around the stem stitching.

3 Use 1 strand of 725 to make straight horizontal stitches across the stem stitching. Keep the straight stitches between the Frixion pen marks, filling from bottom to top. Erase pen marks with an iron.

4 Layer M2 over M1, matching edges. Running stitch around the perimeter with 1 strand of 725 and a $\frac{1}{16}$″ seam allowance.

5 Layer M3 and M4 over the middle, lower section of M2 (see Template M2 for placement). Temporarily lay M7 over top to ensure it will fit between M3 and M4. Remove M7, and running stitch around the perimeter of M3 and M4 with 1 strand of 315 and a 1⁄16″ seam allowance.

6 Layer both M5 pieces on the wings. Running stitch around the perimeter with 1 strand of 310 and a 1⁄16″ seam allowance.

7 Running stitch an M6 piece over each M5 piece with 1 strand of 413. Keep a 1⁄16″ seam allowance.

8 Layer one M7 over the moth, matching edges. Running stitch around the perimeter with 1 strand of 727 and a 1⁄16″ seam allowance.

EMBROIDER LOWER BODY

1 Use a size 3 needle and 6 strands of 316 to stem stitch along the bottom edge of the wings.

2 Draw a line with a Frixion pen below the bright yellow wings (refer to template M1 as necessary). Use 1 strand of 315 to make small straight stitches along the lines. Use an iron to remove pen marks.

3 Use a size 5 needle and 4 strands of 310 to stem stitch along the bottom edge of the bright yellow wings.

4 Use 2 strands of DMC B5200 to satin stitch a small circle with a tail in the middle of each eye spot (M6). The satin stitching should resemble a single quotation mark.

5 Use 3 strands of 315 to stitch straight stitches of various lengths on the inner Mulberry felt pieces.

6 Use 2 strands of 315 to fill in more straight stitches to the same area.

TOP WINGS AND BODY

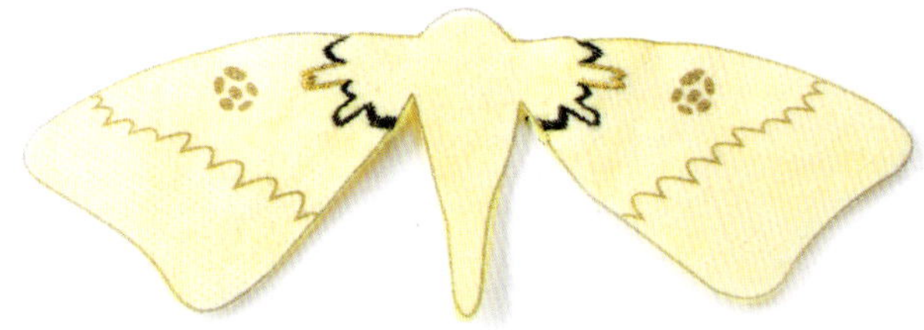

1 Print the Io Moth Wing Pattern onto wash-away paper. Attach to the other M7 piece (see Transferring Templates, page 19).

2 Add straight stitches of various lengths with 1 strand of 310 starting at the inner line of each wing. Use 1 strand of 832 for the largest hump, then switch back to 310 for the rest of the line.

3 Repeat Step 2 for the lower line on each wing using 1 strand and the following order of thread colors: 310, 315, 832, 315, 310.

4 Use 2 strands of 310 to satin stitch the dots on both sides of the wings.

5 Wash away the paper, and let it dry.

6 Blanket stitch appliqué the embroidered M7 over the existing M7 using 1 strand 727.

7 Stitch long straight stitches with 1 strand of 727 to match the bottom of each hump on the wings to the outer edge of the wings.

8 Blanket stitch appliqué M8 over the middle of M7 with 1 strand of 725. Before closing, pad lightly with filling using the stuffing tool.

9 Use a Frixion pen to draw 5 lines across the bottom of the body (refer to template M8 as necessary). Use 2 strands of 832 to stitch short vertical straight stitches along pen marks. Erase the marks with an iron.

TIP: *You may need a larger needle, such as a size 3 or 5 and pliers to help pull your needle through for the last steps.*

10 Create short vertical straight stitches between the Step 9 stitches using 2 strands of 725.

11 In the top area of the body, use 2 strands of 725 to make long and short straight stitches, changing directions of the sections to create roundness (see Template M8 for stitch direction).

12 Make short straight stitches with 2 strands 3078 below the Step 9 stitches. Layer in straight stitches between the Step 11 stitches, following their direction.

13 Use 1 strand 783 to add long and short stitches and straight stitches between the 3078 stitches on the top of the body.

BACK THE HOOP/DISPLAY

Use the 6 ¼" Fig Bellwether felt circle and DMC 3740 to back the hoop (see Hoop Backing, page 38). Insert the hoop in the Modern Hoopla circle frame with black finish. Use cardboard shims to secure.

MOON PHASES

1 Layer Slate M10 pieces over M9 pieces. Use 1 strand of 413 to blanket stitch appliqué together. Use 1 strand of DMC B5200 and blanket stitch appliqué the White M10 piece to the remaining M9 piece. Set aside 1 Slate set (new moon) and the White set (full moon).

2 Layer M11 pieces over 2 sets from Step 1. Use 1 strand of DMC B5200 and blanket stitch appliqué to create two crescent moons. Repeat with M12 pieces to make two half moons and with M13 pieces to make two gibbous moons.

3 Add a thin ring of E6000 on the back of each moon phase and attach to the frame as shown. To ensure that moons are evenly spaced, attach the new moon at the top and the full moon at the bottom. Attach half moons between on each side of the frame, making sure they are mirror images of each other. Place the remaining moons evenly and symmetrically in the remaining spaces.

Blue Mussel with Barnacles

FINISHED PROJECT: 7⅛″ × 10¼″

Although blue mussels are one of the most common bivalve mollusks, their shape and layered colors make them uniquely beautiful. It is the shells' calcitic layers that give them their rich depth and texture. To capture the three dimensionality of the mussel as well as its barnacled environment, this project pushes the boundaries of felt. It transforms flat fibers into a sculptural masterpiece through appliqué layering and heat manipulation.

MATERIALS

5" x 8" oval embroidery hoop
Size 7 embroidery needle
Kai N5000 Scissors
Blue Mussel with Barnacles Templates (page 15)
Quilter's Freezer Paper Sheets
Frixion Heat Erasable Pen
Iron (preferably an Oliso M3 Pro Project Iron)
Hot glue gun and glue
Modern Hoopla Oval Frame (white finish)

THREAD AND FELT

1 sheet 9″ × 12″ Pewter felt
1 sheet 9″ × 12″ Orion Bellwether felt
1 sheet 9″ × 12″ Oxford Blue felt
1 sheet 9″ × 12″ Magpie Bellwether felt
1 sheet 9″ × 12″ Parchment felt
1 sheet 9″ × 12″ White felt
1 sheet 9″ × 12″ Silver felt
1 sheet 12″ × 18″ Cinder felt

DMC six-stranded cotton embroidery floss (1 skein of each)

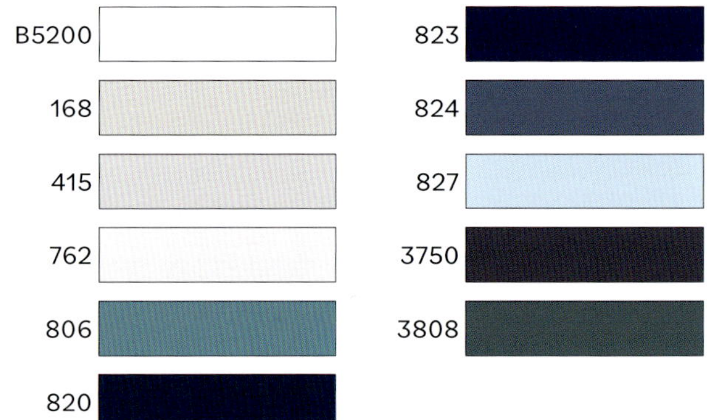

Cut felt pieces for blue mussel

Cut felt pieces for barnacles

CUT LIST

Transfer the Blue Mussel Templates to the felt using freezer paper and a Frixion pen, and cut them out as directed below (see Transferring Templates, page 19). Use the pen for the barnacles, as you will need to cut multiples of the same pieces, and the freezer paper for the rest of the pieces. Cut on the dotted lines of the barnacles. Make sure each piece is labeled.

Background and Backing

Cut 1 oval 6½″ × 9¾″ from Pewter felt (background).

Cut 1 oval 5″ × 8¼″ diameter from Pewter felt (hoop backing).

Blue Mussel

Cut 1 Template M1, M5, M7 and M9 from Orion Bellwether felt.

Cut 1 Template M2, M4 and M6 from Oxford felt.

Cut 1 Template M3, M8 and M10 from Magpie felt.

Cut 1 Template M11 Parchment felt.

Barnacles

Cut 3 Templates B1 and B2 from White Felt.

Cut 2 Templates B3 from White felt.

Cut 3 Templates B1 and B3 from Parchment felt.

Cut 2 Templates B2 from Parchment felt.

Cut 3 Templates B1 from Silver felt.

Cut 2 Templates B2 and B3 from Silver felt.

Cut 1 Template B4, B5 and B6 from Cinder felt.

PREPARE THE HOOP

Place and tighten the 6½″ × 9¾″ Pewter oval into the embroidery hoop. Position the hoop vertically.

FELT APPLIQUÉ BLUE MUSSEL

1 Place M1 in the middle of the felt background with the wide end pointed down. Running stitch around the perimeter with 1 strand of 823. Keep a ⅛″ seam allowance.

2 Layer M2 over M1, aligning edges at the top. Running stitch around the perimeter with 1 strand of 823. Keep a ⅛″ seam allowance.

3 Repeat Step 2 for pieces M3-M11 using 1 strand 3808 for Magpie Bellwether felt pieces, 823 for Oxford and Orion Bellwether felt pieces, and 762 for the Parchment felt piece.

EMBROIDER THE MUSSEL

Refer to the stitch library (page 26) for step-by-step instructions for each embroidery stitch used in this project.

1 Stem stitch around the outside edge of M1 with 3 strands of 823. Stitch along the bottom half of the perimeter only. Stem stitch along the outer edge of M2 only where M2 meets M1 with 3 strands of 3750.

2 Repeat Step 1 for pieces M3- M11, using the following thread for each layer:

M3: 820	M6: 824	M9: 3750
M4: 824	M7: 820	M10: 806
M5: 3750	M8: 824	M11: 827

3 Stem stitch between M2 and M3 (over the running stitch from appliqué) with 3 strands of 824.

4 Repeat Step 3 for the remaining layers, using the following thread in between layers:

M3 and M4: 3750

M4 and M5: 824

M5 and M6: 820

M6 and M7: 3750

M7 and M8: 3808

M8 and M9: 820

M9 and M10: 824

M10 and M11: 3808

M11: 762

Stem stitch in a U-shape for M11, not stitching along the top perimeter.

BACK THE HOOP/DISPLAY

Use 5" × 8 ¼" Pewter felt oval and DMC 168 to back the hoop (see Hoop Backing, page 38). Place the hoop in the Modern Hoopla oval frame with white finish. Use cardboard shims to secure.

BARNACLES

Shaping Barnacles

Fold 1 barnacle diagonally, matching an outer point with an inner point. Run an iron over the fold to create a crease. Create 5 creases for each barnacle, adding the folds one at a time. Crease all barnacles so that they are three dimensional and can stand upright.

Embroider Detail

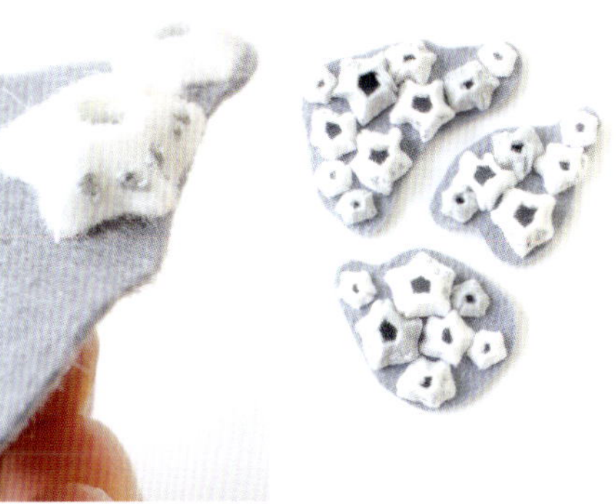

1 For all B2 and B3 Parchment and White barnacles, use 1 strand 168 to make sporadic French knots on two sides. Switch to 2 strands of 168 to sprinkle in more French knots. Repeat for all B2 and B3 Silver barnacles, using 762.

2 Overlap the open ends of each barnacle and hot glue closed.

3 Attach barnacles to B6 with a single whip stitch at the bottom of each of the 5 corners. Use 1 strand of 762 for Parchment barnacles, DMC B5200 for White barnacles, and 415 for Silver barnacles. Repeat for B4 and B5.

Attach to Frame

Hot glue the barnacle-covered pieces around the frame, so that part of them bleeds over into the hoop itself.

Sputnik Sea Urchin with Seaweed

FINISHED PROJECT: 7″ × 7″

On one family vacation at the beach, I spent my days scouring the shore for the perfect seashells. It seemed impossible to find one that had not been broken by the strong waves, or tumbled smooth by the sandy ocean floor. When I did finally find a beautifully intact conch shell, it was very much inhabited, and I tossed back into the water. Years later, my grandma bought my daughters flawless sea urchin shells, and it healed a little piece of young me that never did quite find the perfect seashell. In this project, you will engineer your own faultless urchin, appliquéing dozens of small pieces to build its plump, geometric shell.

MATERIALS

6" embroidery hoop
Size 7 embroidery needle
Kai N5000 Scissors
Sputnik Sea Urchin with Seaweed Templates (page 15)
Quilter's Freezer Paper Sheets (optional)
Frixion Heat Erasable Pen
Iron
Hot glue gun and glue
Modern Hoopla Circle Frame (natural finish)

THREAD AND FELT

1 sheet 12″ × 18″ Tawny Bellwether felt
1 sheet 9″ × 12″ Amethyst Bellwether felt
1 sheet 9″ × 12″ Lilac felt
1 sheet 9″ × 12″ Allium Bellwether felt
1 sheet 9″ × 12″ Linen felt
1 sheet 9″ × 12″ Tortoise Bellwether felt
1 sheet 9″ × 12″ Nori Bellwether felt

DMC six-stranded cotton embroidery floss (1 skein of each)

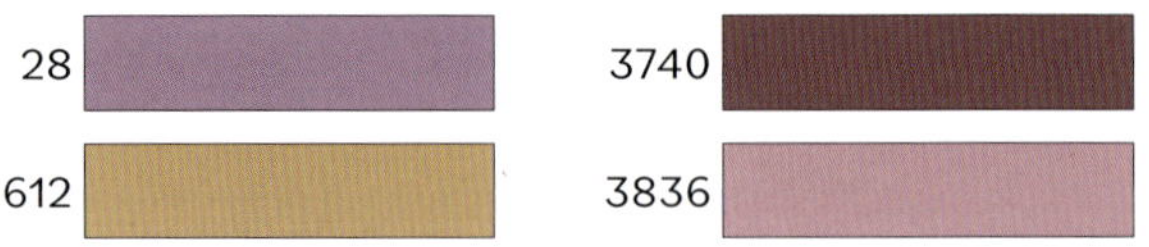

Cut felt pieces for sea urchin and seaweed

CUT LIST

Transfer the Sea Urchin Templates to the felt using your preferred method and cut them out as directed below (see Transferring Templates, page 19). For this project, I suggest using a Frixion pen. Make sure each piece is labeled.

Background and Backing

Cut 1 circle 7″ diameter from Tawny felt (background).

Cut 1 circle 6¼″ diameter from Tawny felt (hoop backing).

Sea Urchin

Cut 5 Templates U1 from Amethyst felt.

Cut 5 Templates U2 from Lilac felt.

Cut 30 Templates U3 from Allium felt.

Cut 30 Templates U4 and U5 from Linen felt.

Seaweed

Cut 1 Template S1 from Tortoise felt.

Cut 1 Template S1 from Nori felt.

Cut 2 Templates S2 from Tortoise felt

Cut 2 Templates S2 from Nori felt.

PREPARE THE HOOP

Place and tighten the 7″ Tawny felt circle into the 6″ embroidery hoop.

EMBROIDER URCHIN PIECES

This sea urchin shell has 5 sections, called *plates* that are made up of U1 and U2 pieces. Each plate has 6 nubs on the outside, called *tubercles*. Tubercles are made up of U3, U4 and U5 pieces. Refer to the Stitch Library (page 26) for step-by-step instructions for each embroidery stitch used in this project.

1 Create a tubercle by stacking U3, U4, and U5 pieces on top of each other, largest to smallest. Place the tubercle in the upper left of U2.

2 French knot in the center of the stack through all layers with 2 strands of 3740.

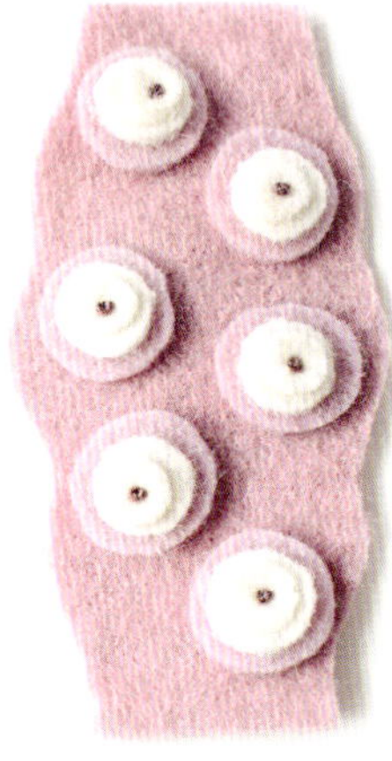

3 Repeat Steps 1 and 2 to add remaining 5 tubercles to U2.

4 Repeat Steps 1–3 to add 6 tubercles to the 4 remaining U2 pieces.

5 With 2 strands of 3836, create 11 French knots around the base of each tubercle. Bring the needle slightly through U3 to keep the tubercle from pulling away from U2. Repeat for the other 4 U2 pieces.

6 Layer U2 over U1, positioning it in the middle. Blanket stitch appliqué with 1 strand of 3740 along the curvy edges of U2. Space stitches close together (about ⅛″ apart).

7 Blanket stitch along the top and bottom of U2 with 1 strand of 3836. This is one finished plate.

8 Repeat Steps 6 and 7 to create the other 4 plates.

ASSEMBLE URCHIN

1 Place two plates together with tubercles facing one another. Back stitch along the outer edge of U1 with 2 strands of 28, keeping a ⅛″ seam allowance.

2 Line the next plate up with the plates from Step 1, keeping the tubercles facing each other. Again, back stitch along the outer edge of U1 with 2 strands of 28, keeping a ⅛″ seam allowance. Repeat to add the next 2 plates.

3 Bring the two edges of the open ring together. Use 2 strands of 28 to back stitch along the outer edge of the U1 pieces. Carefully flip the sea urchin right side out so the tubercles face out.

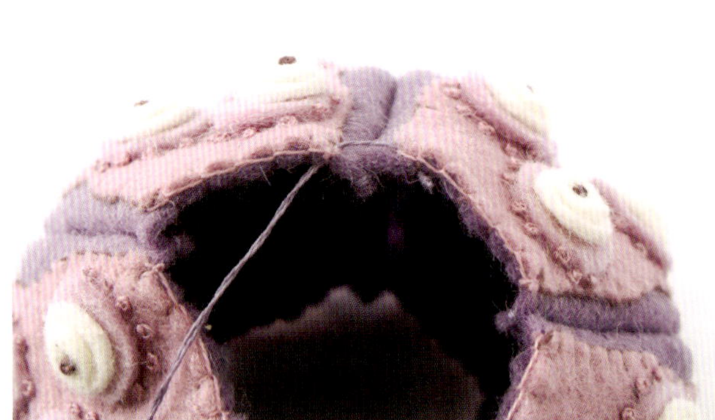

4 Use 2 strands of 28 to straight stitch between the bottom section of U1 on one of the open ends. Pull the corners tight so the U2 pieces touch. Knot off, and snip excess thread. Repeat for all corners.

5 Flip the sea urchin over. Use 2 strands of 28 to weave the needle and thread through the blanket stitching around the entire perimeter of the hole. Pull the thread tightly to cinch the hole. The hole opening should be about ½″ wide.

ATTACH URCHIN TO HOOP

1 Hot glue the perimeter of the smaller hole.

2 Place the sea urchin in the middle of the hoop, glue side down. Press firmly to secure. If you plan to hang this piece on the wall, you may need to add more hot glue just above the hole to keep the urchin from drooping down. This is not necessary if you display the piece flat.

FRAME AND ATTACH SEAWEED

1 Use 6 ¼" Tawny felt circle and DMC 612 to back the hoop (see Hoop Backing, page 38). Place your finished piece into the Modern Hoopla circle frame with natural finish. Use cardboard shims to secure.

2 Gently fold one end of S2 in half lengthways. Run an iron across the fold to create a crease. Continue folding and ironing until you reach the end of the piece. Repeat for all S2 and S1 pieces.

3 Arrange the seaweed pieces around the sea urchin, overlapping and allowing some parts to stick out around the frame. Hot glue the seaweed pieces in place.

about the author

Jenny Bolhofner is a self-taught embroiderer and the artist behind Olive This Felt. She won a coloring contest at a car dealership when she was eight years old, which pretty much secured her future as an artist. Jenny went on to get a BFA in printmaking and drawing at Murray State University in 2010. Four years later, she had her first daughter, Olive, and established her felt business out of a desire to have a creative outlet while being a stay at home mom.

Jenny's work is inspired by observing the world around her and translating that through the layering and experimentation of felt and thread. She enjoys testing the limits of fiber art beyond the traditional realm of two dimensionality.

Jenny has over ten years of experience as a fiber artist, selling her work around the world. Her work has been featured on Canvas Rebel and Create Whimsy. She has published patterns and tutorials with Benzie Design and the DHG Shop, and often teaches workshops at a local art house. She currently resides in Milford, OH, with her husband and two daughters, who are her biggest supporters, but who also think she has too many craft supplies.

You can find her work on Instagram @olivethisfelt and on her website olivethisfelt.com